A Nation of Lords

The Autobiography of the Vice Lords

Second Edition

David Dawley

WAVELAND PRESS, INC.

Prospect Heights, Illinois

For information about this book, write or call:

Waveland Press, Inc.
P.O. Box 400
Prospect Heights, Illinois 60070
(708) 634-0081

To my daughter
Ana Bessy Dawley
Te Quiero

To The Vice Lords
for trust, friendship and protection.

Photographs by David Dawley

"your photography is a record of your living, for anyone who really sees"

Paul Strand

Thanks

For friendship and support during my years on the street, I'm grateful to Bernie Rogers, Frank Monahan, Patrick Murphy, Mike Coffield, Hermon Dunlop Smith, Morrie Leibman, Warren Wiggins, Dick Irish and Judy Ferguson.

For the Doubleday/Anchor Press edition, I was fortunate to have the help of Elsie Simons, Phoebe Monick and Ginger Haight and the advice of Margaret Friedmann, John Erlich and my editor, Loretta Barrett.

For this Waveland edition, my thanks to James Diego Vigil for leading me to my publisher, Neil Rowe, and to Neil for believing in the value of this story.

I'm particularly grateful to Jody Ginsberg for her creativity and technical knowledge in laying out photographs and clippings and to my friend, Brian Porzak, for his help in editing new material. I would also like to thank the staff at Garrett Lab in Washington, D.C. for their care and excellent service in printing the photographs.

For love, even when they haven't understood, thanks to my father and mother, Porter and Dolly Dawley.

Finally, thanks to the Boston Celtics for inspiring me with several decades of buzzer-beating victories — an example to remember when all seems lost and time is running out.

The street gangs of the 70s may not follow the same path as the Vice Lords, but the bitterness, despair and hatred that bred the Lords exist in our cities today. It is captured in this book for all to understand.

Kliatt Paperback Guide

David Dawley did not work with the toughest black gang on Chicago's West Side for two years in order to write this book. He became a Vice Lord for the same reason that he joined the Peace Corps: to put his ideals to the test.

Dawley was on the West Side at the height of the Black Power movement, when whites weren't particularly welcome in the black struggle. But the Vice Lords were powerful enough to assure Dawley's safety (most of the time) and smart enough to realize that a young white activist could be a link to Chicago's business and official powers.

A Nation Of Lords which Dawley wrote after living through the successes and frustration recorded in these pages is the Vice Lord's own story, as known by its only white member.

David Butler
author
The Fall Of Saigon

In 1967 David went into the heart of Chicago's West Side and won acceptance and the respect of one of the toughest gangs in the area. As an outsider and a white he exposed himself to great risks of physical harm, but his efforts and his recorded words, I believe, will make a significant contribution to assisting those who have been the victims of a neglectful society.

A Nation Of Lords will serve as an important social document in understanding and hopefully remedying some of the deep-rooted injustices in our society.

Francis W. Sargent
Governor of Massachusetts

A Nation Of Lords represents some of the best writing on race written in the last twenty years. It recounts the story of Chicago's gang culture and how Dave Dawley helped turn it inside out to help the Lords use their energy and skills to build a new life. *Esquire* magazine called Dawley in 1968, one of "Twenty Seven People Worth Saving." Dawley's book remains one of the books most worth reading.

Dick Irish
author
Go Hire Yourself An Employer

A book of staggering significance, a powerful document that one might call present history. The times it relates have past, but the problems remain, and, indeed, have resurfaced in an even more virulent form. To read the book is to penetrate to the core of the problem.

John A. Rassias
Professor, Dartmouth College

The people down here want to thank you in so many ways for writing a true book about our Nation.

You are all the way down and from all Lords you will be always be known throughout.

King Lewis
Black Gangster Unknown Vice Lords
Stateville Prison

There are tough black street leaders who have emerged as local heroes, and although they are not interviewed on Huntley-Brinkley nor appeal to suburban fund raisers, they are legitimate and powerful. They were street rumblers before the summer of 1965; now they are the new political organizers. They are half guerrilla, half ward heeler. They work between organization and revolution, groping for a way in which a bitter and mobilized minority can change a system they know will never accept them as they are.

Andrew Kopkind
1967

Contents

To Our Fallen Brothers

The Vice Lords have done many things: we've kicked ass, busted heads and made our mamas cry. But we have also improved our community, showed that lives can change and developed hope out of despair.

Lives have been lost; some in gang wars that saw brother fight brother, others in the war to unite brothers. But in whatever ways our brothers have gone down, they died as Lords.

We dedicate our story to these brothers and to the young brothers and sisters, born and unborn, whose story this is.

1972 Introduction

During the late sixties, the energy that street gangs once used in preparation for gang warfare increasingly was directed toward creating viable community organizations.

This story is the evolution of the Vice Lords — the evolution from streetfighting to street corporation, an organizational form of an emerging nation of black youth.

Many have been skeptical about the ability of Vice Lords to move beyond streetfighting, but the qualities that make men company presidents and political leaders are also qualities that lead to success on the street. If Horatio Alger had lived in the ghetto, he might have been a Vice Lord.

The difference between a company president and a Vice Lord is the ghetto. With his brothers of the street a young Vice Lord shares the common experience of deprivation, exploitation, oppression and hopelesssness as the ghetto often leaves the indelible brand of dropout, delinquent, hard-core and unreached. If you are a Vice Lord, there are few second chances and as they say, "After us, there ain't no place to go."

From this experience, black youth have struck back, often in that psychological paradox of self-hatred, by fighting other blacks. The perspective of the street is vital to understanding this past and to developing directions for the future. This book attempts to convey the motivations, attitudes, values, and soul of the streets in Chicago so that the mistakes in Vietnam of attempting to solve social, political, and economic problems with military force alone will not be repeated in this country in the name of law and order.

My personal involvement with the Vice Lords began in the summer of 1967 when I worked in Chicago, for the TransCentury Corporation of Washington, D.C. I had left the country in 1963 shortly after the assassination of John Kennedy, and as an Eagle Scout and Peace Corps Volunteer I had confidence in America's basic values and basic decency. But in 1965 I returned to a country with a war in Vietnam, racial riots in the cities, and emerging scrutiny and disillusionment with government, military, industrial and educational institutions. I watched establishment spokesmen scorn critics and through conspiracy trials perpetuate a national tradition of hanging witches.

When I went to Lawndale, a section of Chicago, I expected to find the hostility that in 1967 demanded that whites leave the black community. Instead I discovered that though Vice Lord leaders understood that white society was exploiting, oppressing and repressing blacks, Bobby Gore reflected the prevailing attitude when he said, "We look at people for what they are."

During the summer, we worked together on research that Trans-Century was conducting for the President's Council on Youth Opportutity, an evaluation of the attitudes of youth in eleven cities toward federally funded summer progams. The research gave me access to the Vice Lords, and during this short period we came to know each other— over the pool table, on the streets at night, at frustrating business meetings, in interviews with youth throughout the West Side. I learned that Vice Lord leaders wanted a change from the traditional dead end street warfare, particularly for the young fellas coming up.

The possibility for building programs seemed real because of two crucial factors: The Vice Lords had street power and the leaders wanted change. Without a powerful organization that already existed and without the commitment of street leaders, a white organizer would not have survived in Lawndale in 1967. Without approval from the Vice Lords no white could have walked where I walked, lived where I lived.

After the summer, I had some ideas for helping the Vice Lords with what they were trying to do. I saw that no one in Chicago was seriously helping the Lords so after a short stint in Washington, partly to explore ideas and resources, I borrowed money, loaded an old Volkswagen and returned to Chicago.

This is not the place for me to discuss my experiences or to elaborate on the process of moving the Vice Lords from gang to community organization. However, in the next two years I became one with the Vice Lords and for anyone to challenge me was to challenge the Vice Lord leaders. Nobody ever knowingly made this challenge. The trust grew very complete, and though I declined, I was offered a voting membership on the nine man board of directors.

When I left Lawndale, after giving three months notice, there was foundation funding of the organization, no leaders were in jail, and there was no street crisis. I felt I had done what I had gone to do, which was not to solve the problems of the ghetto but to help start a process by which a strong street organization could try to improve the community and beyond that attempt to change the conditions in society that perpetuate the colonization of Lawndale.

After a year of organizing, I had the idea for an autobiography of the Vice Lords. The Vice Lord leaders and I agreed that the story should be told, that now was the time and that I should do the book.

The story is both a collection of individual experiences and a composite of experiences and feelings that all Lords share. The book is written from the first person perspective of the Vice Lords. There are direct descriptions from individual Vice Lords and when there is no specific individual speaking, the voice is a composite of many Lords.

My hope is that readers will listen to the story and not think that the book must have been contaminated by a white. The story is actual, not fictional, and the recollections are by street leaders who were there.

It is not completely another story with a happy ending. Despite three years of struggling to learn the white man's paper game, the Vice Lords are still fighting for survival and there is doubt that they will have the opportunity to achieve the potential they have as individuals and inheritors of a nation with liberty and justice for all.

The book ends as life goes on. The quality of that life and ultimately the ending of this story will depend upon how people respond to these voices of the street.

David Dawley
August, 1972

1992 Introduction

I feel that, having survived, I owed something to the dead.

Elie Wiesel

The role of the survivors is to tell the stories of those who haven't survived, and of those who can't tell them on their own, and of those who are still suffering the effects of that long and immensely arduous history.

Louise Erdrich

A Nation Of Lords is a view from the street of an explosive period of urban history — a story that remains instructive about survival in the inner city.

Before the book came out, the Warden of the Cook County Jail relayed a rumor that I'd be killed if the book was published — a message I took as bureaucratic mischief by an administration that wanted to intimidate me. In fact, when I went back to Chicago, a Vice Lord I didn't know whispered: "Don't worry, if anybody starts anything, we're with you — all the way."

I'm proud of *A Nation Of Lords* but more proud of having worked in the front lines of the sixties. I had studied guerrilla warfare as a Peace Corps Volunteer in rural Honduras, and while in Chicago, I sometimes thought that my work as a community organizer reflected comparable adventure and dedication to change. After more than twenty years, I still prefer to talk about our work rather than my personal experiences, but the truth is that at the peak of Black Power, I was one of a few whites in the country working and living in a hard core inner city.

Friends wondered about my sanity and worried about my safety; black detectives didn't think any outsider — even black — could be accepted, and black nationalists were surprised to find me late at night at Vice Lord headquarters. Fats Crawford, a leader of the Deacons For Defense said, "You're a privileged dude — there just aren't any whites that come around here."

Nevertheless, during two years of living on the first floor of what the *Sun Times* described as "Chicago's bloodiest corner," I organized what were considered to be the most violent outcasts of the ghetto into a constructive community force. Remembering these years is painful because many friends are dead, but I refuse to have researchers, politicians or journalists who weren't there ignore what we achieved, write off what we accomplished as a liberal experiment or diminish our success by remembering only the South Side gangs.

Some of my Vice Lord friends worried that I'd "turn white" when I left Chicago. Safe in a suburb, would I be as "black" as I was in Chicago in 1968? Would I deny what they had allowed me to become? My obligation to these friends is to keep telling the story of how a street gang became a community organization that turned a violent neighborhood into Head Start's most improved block. Even though some may not understand, to say I'm a Vice Lord honors their friendship and trust.

Although I felt safe, Sixteenth and Lawndale was a dangerous corner. Out of thirty friends, I was the only one who two years later hadn't been shot, cut, wounded or killed. My first apartment was set on fire; I had a gun pointed to my head and my car was shot, but when the West Side rioted after Martin Luther King was killed, I walked through the flames with tape recorder and camera. I was a Vice Lord, a registered voter in the infamous Twenty Fourth Ward and at home in Chicago's Vietnam.

Recently, I was interviewed in "Eyes On The Prize," the television history of civil rights, because in 1966 I was with the Meredith March in Greenwood, Mississippi when the Student Nonviolent Coordinating Committee first used the phrase, "Black Power," a turning point in the movement as many young blacks turned away from nonviolence.

A year later, I was an organizer in one of the baddest black ghettos in the country — a tenth generation WASP whose ancestors landed in Newburyport, Massachusetts and later moved by ox sled to Bath, New Hampshire. Like my ancestors, I've taken the road less traveled. Nevertheless, when the road took me to Lawndale, even Vice Lords wondered what a nice white boy like me was doing in a neighborhood where a corner tavern was known as the "Bucket of Blood."

One researcher has described this period as "naive," — just what I was called in the Peace Corps before organizing townspeople to develop credit unions and build a health clinic that still serves poor campesinos thirty years later.

The simple truth is that the Vice Lords and I came together because I was hired to conduct research about summer programs, and we stayed together because we liked each other and I couldn't walk away without leaving too much of myself behind.

There was no formal evaluation of what we did, but results were obvious: there was less crime, fewer homicides, "grass where there was glass" and storefront programs that served the community. Residents walked freely, business owners appreciated safer streets, and young men dared to dream.

Unfortunately, as I describe in "Nothin Left But Death," these changes didn't survive the seventies. My hope is that if truth and memory are passed along, there may be inspiration and commitment to try again.

David Dawley
January, 1992

A Nation of Lords

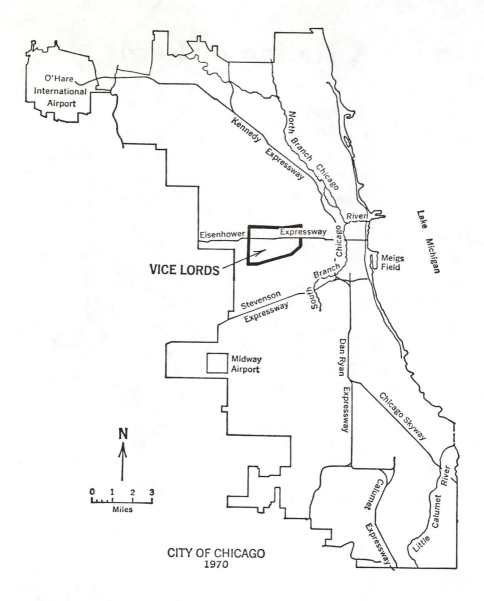

O'Hare
International
Airport

Kennedy Expressway

North Branch Chicago

River

Lake Michigan

Eisenhower   Expressway

VICE LORDS

Branch Chicago

Meigs
Field

Stevenson
Expressway

South 4th

Dan Ryan Expressway

Midway
Airport

Chicago Skyway

Calumet River

N

0 1 2 3
Miles

Calumet Expressway

Little Calumet River

CITY OF CHICAGO
1970

1958

It's Your World; I'm Just Livin' in It

When we got here, the pattern was already laid out for us. We weren't aware of what was going on and what we thought, but we were living in the years when you couldn't walk the streets without somebody telling you they were gonna down you.

Much of what we did was bad, but we didn't know why, and there just wasn't anybody who could help us. Now we know something about what made us kill each other, but in 1958 we were crammed so close together that the least little thing could touch something off.

We've got three hundred thousand people in Lawndale and seventy thousand people in one square mile where there used to be only ten thousand. Until the late fifties Lawndale was a middle-class Jewish neighborhood, but people panicked when blacks began moving in, and as the Jews moved out, real estate brokers bought houses one week for fourteen thousand dollars and sold them to blacks the next week for twenty-six. The only way people could afford to live there was to divide up the houses and make apartments. A place is designed to hold just so many people, but in our hoods, everything gets jammed up. You have two or three families in one six-room apartment. When this was white, there was just one family in the same space.

Elzy is a twenty-year-old Vice Lord and the first home that he can remember was stone ghetto, stone slums.

"The buildings were old bullshit rundown coal stove buildings; the stoves were never hot; and there were no bannisters on the stairs. There was no central heating or all that aristocratic shit, just a big potbellied stove in the middle of the floor.

"We had a roll-out couch and in the wintertime we'd pull that motherfucker as close to the stove as she could stand it. I was about ten years old and I slept with my two oldest sisters, and my brothers slept on the floor. This is how the honkies did us."

3

By 1960 Lawndale was in the top 20 percent of neighborhoods in Chicago in infant mortality, population receiving welfare, unemployment and overcrowding of housing for families with income under three thousand dollars.

Most of the people in Lawndale never had anything and when the fellas were coming up, there was nothing to do. The kids that are still under mama's wings may go into the recreation buildings, but eventually they will be turned out for younger kids, and there's nothing to accommodate them.

"Livin' in this shit, ain't nothin' for 'em to do but drink and start fightin' each other. They don't have no reason except that they live in the ghetto and don't have nothin' to do. And if you look for somethin' to do, you look for somethin' wrong to do.

"Get up in the morning, you know maybe we're gonna tear up something, but nothing is decided until you get with everybody else.

"Most of the time even the leader had nothin' planned. You sit around a porch, a doorway, on a step, in a gangway, get high, mess over somebody, stomp 'em, kick 'em, cut 'em, you didn't care. It was fun to you."

The day is mostly quiet and there were times when cats didn't even come out of the house until four in the evening. Usually if you had anything you wanted to do wrong, you did it at night. The night was for prowling, gang rumbles, getting high at parties, boogalooing, anything you wanted. Many times we didn't go to bed until the sun came up, and almost always we were up until three or four in the morning. We were just walking, talking, bullshitting and drinking. Nobody went to bed.

The gang was a family to all street cats. The gang fed him, gave him initiative, responsibility and respect, which the system didn't give him because he was born poor. Born poor, you dig? Not just black. You got Puerto Rican, Chinese, and poor whites who tell the same story.

With the overcrowding, there were not enough playgrounds, schools or parks, and fights began over who could use whatever there was. Gangs were strong because they controlled schools, controlled swimming pools, controlled movie theaters, controlled baseball diamonds, controlled park areas. In the summer, everybody had to be in a gang to enjoy things. Had to be a gang to go swimming, had to be a gang to go to the movie, had to be a gang to go to a dance. Had to because gangs controlled all of these areas. The gang was survival. If you weren't in a gang and you went to these areas, you got dusted.

Bobby Gore was born in the Cook County Hospital and he was raised in the Maxwell-Halsted Street section, the heart of Jewtown, a neighborhood where the residents were mostly black but the businesses were predominantly Jewish.

"I was about nine years old and we started out fighting all because of a baseball game. We had a baseball team that was called the Baby Dragons and then the Vikings. It seemed that in every neighborhood we went to for a baseball tournament, you had to fight to get out. Sometimes even if we lost we had to fight. It was actually a social-athletic club, but after what happened so many times, we decided we would be on our p's and q's for the next time. Win, lose, or draw, we would be ready for the fight, and that was gonna be the most important thing.

"After a while they labeled us a gang and we started recruiting to put a certain amount of protection on ourselves from other gangs."

In order to protect himself a guy had to be involved in what was going on in the street. If a guy goes out of his neighborhood and they know that all the fellas on his street stick together, then he has some protection.

As Bobby says, "If I were going down to Kedzie and I don't have any friends up there, I'd make it my business to try and meet somebody that was involved and I'd go out of my way to try to get involved myself. Not saying that I would get misused, but when you come up on the street and you got fifteen to twenty cats that know you and speak to you, you feel kind of good on the inside, you feel at ease. But if you didn't know anybody and you go up there, you're gonna be shakin' in your boots."

When Bobby was about sixteen he moved from Jewtown to Lawndale. He used to go back to his old neighborhood every day, but, slowly, he met a few Lawndale fellas and started drifting away from Jewtown.

"I met a few more guys and we formed a singing group called the Clevertones. We used to practice at BBR, a social center, and this was the place where the Clovers had meetings. This was the club that dominated the area.

"Through singing and making appearances, I got a chance to meet a lot of those guys. Some were from my old neighborhood and knew the type cat I was, so they invited me to join. A younger brother of a guy that sang with us was one of the chiefs in the Clovers and this brought a closeness between the club and the singing group.

"Eventually the whole singing group joined the Clovers, and we said we were the Clevertones, the Clovers singing group."

In the days of the Clovers, roughly from 1951 until about 1956, nobody was forced to join. A guy would join simply to have something to identify with and to put a little protection around himself. They never had any recruiting where they would go out and beat up a guy and say you better join. The involvement pulled the younger cats in, not the muscle. Like when a cat would drop out of school and he has no place to go, he would come up on Sixteenth Street and see a group of guys hanging around. Every day he comes up, he sees a particular group of guys, and eventually he wants in. This would give him something to do rather than be a loner on the corner.

"The Clovers had also started off as a baseball team and social club and just kept growin' and growin' and growin'. They used to give dances and there were other clubs in the neighborhood that didn't care for the Clovers, simply because we paid dues to the club. We had sweaters and emblems and threw our own parties.

"Quite naturally, we weren't gonna let anybody come off the street and destroy our thing, so whenever two or three toughies come in and felt like they were going to run something, we'd put 'em out. And we'd put 'em out the way they wanted to go. If a cat wanted to go because we asked him, this was well and good. If he wanted to box, this was well and good. And if he wanted to get shot out of the place, he could have got that."

Another Vice Lord, The Goat, came from California when he was twelve and, like Bobby, he learned that he needed protection. Within two weeks he was approached in the street by ten boys, and the leader challenged him:

"Say, where you goin'?"

"I'm goin' to the store."

"Well, this here is the Braves, Jack, we run it. Now give us a quarter."

Well, Goat had never seen a gang, so he said, "What you mean you run it?"

"They took my quarter, beat me in the nose, flipped me down, and I went home."

"So I asked a cat how do I become a member of the Van Dykes, another gang in the neighborhood, and he say you gotta fight one of the baddest cats in the club and even if you lose, long as you give a good thumpin', you can become a member.

"I went home and thought about it. Do I fight this dude and become a member, or do I just don't fight him and be a rebel? Then I thought that rebels can't go to the show, can't go to the beach, can't go to house parties, can't have no girlfriends and walk the street.

"I went back and said, 'OK, Jack, I'll thump one of the tough cats.' So they picked the cripple boy. His name was Joe Tappey and he was a helluva rassler. Don't think they picked him to make it easy for me to win; he had strength in his arms, and one of his friends told me the only way you can whip him is to stay off him and punch.

"'Don't get up under him 'cause if you do and he gets his arms on you, throw your chips in 'cause you out of it.'

"We fought two days later after school. I stayed away from him and I jabbed him and punched him. We punched for about twenty-five, thirty minutes. Finally he got his arms around me and that was about the end of the fight.

"After the fight I was a member."

When the Vice Lords started to come up, the average kid in a gang wasn't out to kill another cat in a gang. The struggle was for reputation, not for killing. The game was to see who was the toughest, the baddest, to see who was the boss. At that time, the boss was the best fighter and the slickest, the cat that had the most control and respect in the group.

We almost bred fighting. We used to get together fifteen to twenty guys in a vacant lot and rassle or box all day long. If one guy was tougher than the other, we'd put two and three guys on the tough one to see what he could do, to make sure that he could handle himself. It was like watching a guy fight the lions.

There was nothing like a good ass whippin'. You even enjoyed getting whipped when you thought it was a fair whipping. The more whippings you got, the more reputation you got. You didn't get big just by how many you won or lost; you got big also by how many challenges you made. If a guy knew you fought Stump Daddy of the Cobras, he knew you was badder than he was because he didn't even try.

If you were in a gang and wanted a reputation, you got to whip a guy with a reputation. So you prepare yourself for him. Before you challenge the toughest cat, you took on twenty or thirty others, just like in the days of cowboys. Before a cowboy became the fastest gun, he had to challenge and build a name.

In those days, there wasn't a lot of shooting and a switchblade knife or baseball bat would pop up now and then, but mostly you'd go from the nubs. We didn't care about money (your daddy paid the rent and your mama bought your clothes) and we never worried about policy or protection, because that was the syndicate. We enjoyed parties, swimming pools, going to movies, and collecting girls, but fighting was the name of the game.

Our motivation was to be the baddest, toughest, roughest gangbanger, or streetfighter, and what showed a cat was powerful was turf. We needed land to establish our identity and we really didn't own land. But we thought this was ours and we paraded the streets and occupied certain corners.

We would have corners where we got to check out anybody who comes through that we don't know. We would walk up and say:

"Who is you and where's your crib?"

He say, "Down there," and somebody beat him up side the head and kick his motherfucking ass.

Or you would tell a cat, "Well, dig, man, I want the movie."

He say, "I ain't gonna give it to you. If you gonna take it, I'll be at the show next Sunday."

That's an automatic challenge, so next Sunday whoever runs whoever out of there runs the movie. Then the word spreads that so-and-so took the show from so-and-so.

Next you take the swimming pool, then the park, then two blocks, three blocks, until he doesn't have any territory at all. The only thing left for him to do is to become a member or move out of the area.

This happened to Cupid, who began as a Morphine and later became a Vice Lord.

"I was always the drifter, always by myself. I had a few friends that was in the gangs and we'd be together sometimes — pitchin' pennies, shootin' dice, and different things — but they never jumped on me.

"Then I moved and that's when I got whipped and beat for just comin' to school. I couldn't eat my lunch 'cause they took my money, and when I did get my lunch, some bigger fellas would reach over in my plate and get my meat while some other guy takes my milk.

"So I learned what a gang was. This was the Harlem School, and the Imperial Chaplains and Comanches ran that set. When they started jumpin' on me, I moved and got a transfer to Lawson School. But then the Cobras and the Morphines start jumpin' on me. Each group always stayed around some school, so instead of movin' again, I joined the Morphines.

"Eventually we got into it with the Lords and one night we was givin' a dance and from the dance we was gonna roll on the Lords.

"But while we was gettin' together, the Vice Lords rolled down on us and there wasn't no escape. They had stole cars, got out, and come in from all ways.

"We had a thing called the Snake Pit where no other gangs was supposed to come and be able to get out. But the Lords edged and nobody expected them to come down there on us, since we planned to go down there at them.

"They came in on us, whipped us up, and took our president over in the park and talked to him. He became a Vice Lord so I knew right then it was time for me to get with the Lords—no sense in trying to keep with the Morphines and they steady losin' and I'm steady gettin' whipped.

"So I got with the Lords. They had whipped a whole lot of us—broke my leg, broke my arm, put me in the hospital—but after I got in the Lords, I began to love 'em and it was worth giving my life for. And any time, even today, if a Lord come to me for some help and I know he's a Lord, I gotta go because I love 'em.''

If We Can't Get along, Then We Gonna Get It On

The Vice Lords started in 1958 in the St. Charles reformatory, where seven fellas decided to form a new club. The founder of the club, Peppilow, had actually thought of the idea before going to St. Charles. He had gone to a meeting of the Imperial Chaplains to be initiated, but when he walked in, Big John said, "We don't want no punk motherfucker in the organization."

"Big John just didn't dig me or somethin' and he really didn't even know me. Say I wasn't vicious enough, you know, I wasn't no terrible dude."

Pep stayed around and tried to work into the Imperials through his friend Calloway, but he was never accepted, so he drifted off and started running with two or three young dudes.

"I had left my house at the age of fourteen and started a group called the Phantom Burglars. We used to burglarize to live because I was livin' on my own. That went on for about a good year without me gettin' busted. Then I got busted and the Phantom Burglars were sent away. I was sent to the Illinois State Training School for Boys, known as St. Charles."

Pep was tall and big, fast on his feet and quick with his hands. He was about fifteen, six foot one, and 190 pounds. He played football, basketball and baseball and he was a fast, tough boxer. Very few could box him and he became known as the big drum around the institution.

When guys came from the street "on the new," Pep checked them out. One day his ace, Leonard Calloway, was in the line. Calloway was a tall, thin, dark-skinned dude, real neat. He wasn't a real humbugger, but he was treacherous. He was known for stepping out of gangways on you when you're walking home or going to a party. If you didn't outrun him, he'd shoot you — shotgun or pistol, sometimes both. He always kept one of the two.

10

Pep was tickled to see Calloway and arranged to have him assigned to the same cottage. Most of the dudes in the institution had jobs such as clerks, so everything that was done in the institution was done by the inmates one way or another. The original seven Lords all had good jobs and through these jobs they controlled what happened at St. Charles. Pep was number one butcher, Calloway was number two. Toehold was number one in the kitchen and Ralph Bonds was number two. Maurice Miller was an Honor Boy and another guy was in the linen room.

With Toehold in the kitchen, "if there was a cat around that we don't dig, we make him cut on out. We tell him we'll put him on bones," and whoever was on bones didn't eat like the rest of the fellas. All the Lords got new clothes, and the other cats got pants that had been worn three or four times.

The original seven had not all known each other before St. Charles, but they got tight by having meetings when the regular house parents were off and the substitutes were on. This was twice a week and Pep remembers laying down in the basement and talking about gangbanging.

"I wasn't in a gang at that time so I hit on Cal: 'Say, we ought to start somethin' of our own'. Calloway said beautiful so we started. We put two candy bars up at club meetings and if anybody talked out of line, he'd put up another. That's what you call 'the store,' so when we got together, we'd all eat together, and the cottage parents didn't know what was going on."

When the club started, there were different impressions about what the Vice Lords were. Maurice Miller thought the club was for social activities; Calloway thought they were going to stay tight with the Imperials but just have a club of their own; and since both Wren and Cal belonged to the Imperials, the Imperials assumed that they would be tight with the Lords. But Pep was the leader and he didn't give a damn about the Imperials.

"I had a personal vendetta to settle with the Imperials, especially Big John. That's right, I wanted to get 'em. And eventually the humbug did go down with the Imperials and nobody really know why it started. All they know, I just say it's war with the Imperials."

At first the name was Conservative Lads, then Imperial Vice Lords. But Pep didn't like the Imperial part because they had iced him, so Conservative was added to Vice Lords. Calloway had thought of the Vice and Lord because he had seen these words and looked them up in the dictionary. When he found that "vice" meant having a tight hold (keeping it tight and not letting go), that was it.

Maurice Miller had wanted Conservative because he and about five of his partners were conservative-type dudes. Maurice used to wear the tight pants back in fifty-eight that became popular several years later. He was the first one to get out of St. Charles and he was supposed to start it off, so Conservative was added for his sake. But Vice Lords was quicker to say and the way the club developed, Conservative didn't make any sense, so this was not well known until after 1964.

Gradually, one by one, two by two, the seven got out of St. Charles. They started going to dances, then giving dances, and guys wanted to join because there were always lots of broads. If they checked out, they were let in.

Then other gangs began jumping on the younger cats and they came back bloodied up and said the Imperials jumped on them, or the Cobras jumped on them, or somebody else jumped on them. The older fellas just got tired of that and decided to take care of business for them.

When Pep got out he said, "Well, let's get together," and he brought in some of his friends — Son, Wren, Trip, Green and his cousin, Sloop. Like Cal, Son stayed pretty clean. He wore a gangster hat and a white trenchcoat all the time. He was treacherous but he was also a thumper — either way, didn't make any difference how he went. Guys gave him respect when they saw him. Wren was a maniac, a killer. He wasn't as big as Pep, about 175 pounds, but he was one of the few that would box him: they used to dust each other for fun.

The first combat for the Vice Lords was with the Clovers. Pep, Trip, George Haggart, Wren, and Big Lord went to a party in K-Town, a section of the West Side where several streets begin with the letter K. Pep was going with a girl who was giving a party and about four Clovers started a humbug.

"We whipped them four so they split. Then when we was in there messin' with the girls — laughin' and jokin' — the doors were kicked open and about fifty to sixty Clovers came back in saying 'One Clover fight, all Clovers fight'.

"They hemmed us up in a corner, so we got to fightin'. My friend Trip was knocked out, layin' in the closet. Myself, I had a scraper that you scrape up snow with and I was hemmed up in the alley. Wren had to run off and left one of his shoes, so I was about the last one.

"They had me hemmed up and everybody was saying 'Get him, get him,' so I fought for a while, you know, and by that time I saw a way to split. I was about twelve blocks from my crib so I broke through the gangway. They chased me past my house, and my sister saw them, so the second time around, I got a chance to get into the crib.

"The next day I called all seven together and say we gotta grow in order for us to be even with them dudes."

The first target for takeover was the Barons, another little club. There were about twenty-four of them, and Pep went to Farragut High School to pick a humbug with them.

"It took us about a week to dust 'em and make 'em join the Vice Lords. We got 'em jammed up tight and told 'em instead of goin' ahead, why don't they come on and join us since we're the strongest. Ain't no sense in them tryin' to make it on their own, because they can't make it."

The Barons had been jumped on by the Clovers, the Imperials, and the Cobras, so the Barons just dropped their name and became Vice Lords.

Another group, the Van Dykes, combined with the Lords after only a two-day war. The president of the Van Dykes found out his brother was vice president of the Vice Lords, and he said he wouldn't fight because he wasn't out to kill his own brother.

After a year of constant day-to-day humbugging, the Lords had two to three hundred for a fight and Pep's name began to ring. But still we had to grow. We wanted new territory. We needed movie theaters and swimming pools that the Cobras had, a better park or a bigger theater, or the other side of a street because five broads lived there. These were the profits of turf and breaking up other gangs, and the further we reached, the sweeter the fire became.

What made us so powerful was that we always fought two or three gangs at one time. We fought the Egyptian Cobras on the west; the Comanches, Imperial Chaplains, and Continental Pimps on the east, and there wasn't much happening in the south or northwest. We never believed in uniting with a group. If they couldn't change their names to Vice Lords, we couldn't unite with them.

When we started breaking up groups, we looked for them everywhere, caught 'em, and dusted 'em. We try to find them on the way home because there has always been a thing about trying to find out where the enemy stays and what the enemy likes to do.

There would be Lords who got together every night to catch one, two, or three other dudes—"put some hurtin' on 'em and then go back and let them spread the word to their fellas. Just enough hurtin' so they understand they don't run nothin'.''

Sometimes the police would get a call and they wouldn't come until it was over because we were out there.

When we recruited we asked a dude if he wanted to become a Lord. We'd tell him we wanted him to do this or do that. If he says "I wantta be a Lord," he was a Lord. That's all it took then: anything walkin' or talkin' could become a Lord. Some would say, "My friends left the Cherokees and joined the Vice Lords so I left"; others that "everyone needs a group and all my friends are Lords." But if a dude says "No, I can't be no Lord," he got his ass whipped right then and there, and everytime we see him we gonna whip his ass 'til he change his mind and say he's gonna be a Lord. Eventually they would want to join.

Everybody in the club used to box, and everyone could box good. Pep and Cal taught Toehold in St. Charles and when they wanted somebody dusted, Toe would handle it.

"We used to get us two or three pints of wine, go down the street, and say which one wantta knock this cat out first. We just pick any cat, don't nobody got to know him. We don't know whether he can box or not and we didn't care. Sometimes we used to argue about whose turn it is to knock him out.

"Some of the fellas would go to jail for a couple months and come back pretty heavy, so we would tell him to fire on the biggest dude comin' down the street — anybody except old people; we didn't mess with no old people. So we tell him, 'If you so heavy, there he is, fire on him.' Not knock him down, kick him, and stomp him, just fire on him.''

But there were also fellas who just jumped on anybody — fellas like Cupid.

"I jumped on a lot of people for nothin'. Didn't do nothin' to me or our club, but I was lettin' 'em know what would happen if they did. Some of the others we kept fightin' to keep them from thinkin' they could take over.''

※ ※ ※

In 1959, when he was about sixteen, Pep was cracked again and sent back to St. Charles. The Lords weren't at peace with anybody, so everybody that went into St. Charles was fighting the Vice Lords, and everybody that walked in with a different name was considered an enemy.

With Pep in St. Charles, the Imperial Chaplains got the Imperial

Knights and started catching some of the Lords. One day they caught two of the fellas, Pep's sister, and a girl Pep was going with. A dude named Bow Chest slapped and beat Pep's girl, and a new arrival at St. Charles told Pep.

Pep wanted to know what hand Bow Chest slapped her with and when he found out he told the fellas in the institution that he was going on a week's vacation, ''and when I come back, I'm gonna bring Bow Chest's arm with me.''

Pep called his people together and found out the Imperials were giving a party. But his wires were crossed and half the fellas went one place and half went to another party. When Pep got to the right party, the Imperials were there.

''They fell on us that time and they did a pretty good job of it, so we split and rather than going back right then, I called a meeting for the next day at Gregory School.

''I skin it down to the fellas that we're goin' to a place where we know they won't be so we all can get together and get that love for each other.''

For two days they just traveled to the beaches, forest preserves, and Riverview, the amusement park. Just traveling, living together, staying away from the Imperials.

On the next Friday, they found out through some girls that the Imperial Chaplains were hanging in the Central Park show about two to three hundred strong. Pep told all the dudes that couldn't stand it with the fists to split. There were about fifty Lords, and Pep was in the front.

''We was walkin' down Roosevelt and we had to go about twelve blocks. When we got about eight blocks, there was only about forty of us. When we got to six blocks, there was only about thirty of us. When we got about two blocks from the show, there was about twenty of us, and when we got to the show and the Imperials came out, there was twelve of us.

''I told the fellas, 'Say, man, you ain't been humbuggin' right. This is do or die.'' So myself, Wren, Trip, McLamore, Bate, Stucky, Toehold, Yancey, and Big George stood up to the Imperials and they rolled down on us. We saw that we couldn't run, and the girls was there, so we humbugged.

''It was a good eighty or ninety of 'em humbuggin'. The rest was just standin' there laughin'. We fought for about ten or fifteen minutes and the tide began to change: the Imperials surely but slowly began fading back. We dusted 'em so they fell back into the show.

"We was leavin' and got about a block away when all the show came out. There were about 150 of them then and they caught Wren who was straggling behind. One of the fellas told me the Senior Imperials had got Wren—Wren was about sixteen and these were dudes four, five years older than he was—so I told the fellas to get some bricks, bottles, knives, anything they had.

"We went back to get Wren. They had him against the wall, swingin' on him, so we started throwin' them bottles and they started duckin'. We just went into 'em and start oilin' 'em. We just started actin' crazy, like we was madmen. They tried to go back up into the show, but Wren say, damn this, and we followed them all up into the show and got to humbuggin'.

"Now this dude, Bow Chest, was comin' out of the show, so McLamore and I grabbed his arm and we was cuttin' his arm off and cuttin' him all up. When we got his arm halfway off, the police rolled down on us.

"We went to court and somehow they had stitched the arm back on Bow Chest. But he was cut all around the head and we had branded him in the back: CVL."

Pep was sent back to Charleytown and the word was out that he had nearly cut off the dude's arm. The papers had said the Lords were a monstrous, vicious group, so all the Imperials that were in St. Charles quit the Imperials and became Vice Lords. There were still young dudes on the street in the Imperial Knights but the Imperials were nearly gone.

✄ ✄ ✄

Everybody wants to pull with the winning side, so more members came in whenever five or six Lords turned out a party or dusted some other group. There were also dudes who just liked the way we were dressing with black capes and gold lettering and an earring in one ear.

Cupid was scared to get a hole punched in his ear even though he had been beat and cut many times.

"They brought out this earring that you just clamp on and it pierces your ear, but it didn't go through the front so I went on and let a girl pierce it. I was afraid of shots from the doctor so I couldn't see nobody stickin' a needle straight through my ear. I had her put ice on it and rub it and carry on."

Calloway had designed the Vice Lord symbol of top hat, cane, and gloves. He used canes to spell out "CVL" and he had a skeleton head with a top hat, bow tie, and a cigarette holder with smoke coming from the skull. The capes were symbols of the Lords, and sometimes the police came up and made the fellas take them off (they were ideal for hiding a shotgun or baseball bat). A cape cost twenty-one dollars and the fellas that could afford them wore them. Some wore them on the weekend and those that had more than one wore them during the week: Calloway even had one made of cashmere.

The Lords were tough now and everybody trembled when they heard the cry of "Mighty, Mighty Vice Lawd!!" After breaking up the Spanish Counts and the Bandits, we even had a curfew on the streets. At 9 P.M. all gangs were supposed to be in their cribs. We had spies and when we found out that somebody wasn't in the crib, we'd go around and make an example out of him. They couldn't be in the park or on the porch; they had to be in the house. If they weren't, they got a whippin'.

We still didn't have one single hood. We stayed in one set for a while, usually until the police ran us away, then moved to another corner. For a year most of the meetings were held in the basement of a building at 2135 South Millard that was owned by Pep's mother. Then we moved to the Douglas Park boathouse. Normally these meetings were just to see what was going on. There were one or two hundred people, and after the meetings, we had dances.

Every now and then somebody would say let's collect some money, so we would charge twenty-five cents a week dues. A neighborhood preacher was keeping the money for us, but when there were about six hundred dollars, the Reverend ran off and sent us a Christmas card from Florida. Generally though, the only dues were that you be at the club meeting. If you weren't, then you had a punishment, and the punishment was either the belt line or to fight somebody that could dust you.

Most of the fights weren't planned and there were only a few large ones. We had groups of thirty-five or forty dudes who would check out the hoods and by bumping into another gang, there would be a gangbang. One of those times was at Elks Hall on Ogden and Trumbull where seven Vice Lords fought the Cobra Nation in what Calloway calls the greatest fight of the century on the West Side.

The Lords were Calloway, Big James, C. Archie, Toehold, Big Hercules, Billy Washington, and one other. When they fell into Elks Hall, Calloway counted sixty to seventy Cobras in the dance hall.

The Cobras had a symbol, a rubber snake, and when they throw the rubber snake on the floor, it's a humbug. But when Gray Ghost threw the snake on the floor, Calloway caught him and dusted him.

"We had umbrellas with the handles filled with lead that we melted down in 'em, and that's what I dusted Gray Ghost with. I made him pick up the snake, so they copped out. There were only about twelve of them then, but we slipped and let one of them sneak out for the rest of the Cobras.

"When we got outside, I looks across the street and say, " 'Yeah; here come the Mighty Vice Lawds,' and I holler, 'Mighty Vice Lawd!'

"My response was 'Yo ho, Mighty Cobras!'

"We couldn't get no hat so we had to thump. There were a lot of snakes out there, a lot of snakes. And the law was there, but since there were no knives and guns involved, they just stood by. That's what made it so sweet. There were swollen jaws and nest eggs, knots on the head, and I had a knot on top of a knot.

"The law finally broke it up, but I had a beaver hat, the first hat I ever bought — I paid thirty dollars for that hat — and when I found out that was gone, I really went berserk. All the Cobras on the other side of the street bunched up and I raced across the street into the crowd and asked for Stump Daddy, one of the Cobra chiefs. They called him Stump Daddy 'cuz he put some stumps on a nigger's ass if he caught 'em. He was about five foot eight and two hundred pounds.

"I asked him where was my hat and he say he didn't know. I say somebody got to get up off my hat, otherwise this is not over with (I know now that my fellas is on the way, and sure 'nough, they was comin' from everywhere). I did get my hat back but not that night. Pocahontas, one of the young ladies, was sweet on me and she kept the hat. That was the only way we could get together.

"Pocahontas and another girl, Crazy Connie, were Cobraette leaders. Everybody was hittin' on Crazy Connie but she never turned Vice Lady. We had "killin' floors" in basements or vacant storefronts where we put mattresses, couches, and chairs.

"Even though Pocahontas lived in K-Town, we went together for quite a while. I had to sneak out there and sneak back, and when we broke up, I went by there on a Sunday and asked her if she would come on the back porch. She came out on her back porch and I went down in her backyard and got me a stick and dug in the yard. I came up with a double-barreled shotgun wrapped in plastic and I looked up and told her:

"'Say, we through now, baby; I just wanted to let you know the times I was comin' over here I wasn't so love-struck that I was willing to get my head cracked just to come see you. This was for your fellow members if they ever confronted me out here.'

"So I come on through the gangway, got in the car, and pulled off. I got a lot of information from that young lady. I did a lot of reading and found out that any man's weakness is a woman, but I used that to my own advantage."

The big fights came after several humbugs like Elks Hall. When somebody got really fed up with another group, the toughest guys in the club would talk to the war counselor. Calloway was war counselor for the Lords because he knew strategy and how to make sneak attacks. If he and Pep decided to roll, lieutenants would go around and tell the fellas to meet in the park.

If the meeting was for seven and there were five segments of Lords north of the park, the fifth segment would leave at six and go through the other sets until they became a body. Once everyone was together, they would march to meet the other gang. On the way they would discuss what they were going to use — knife, brass knuckles, whatever — and they're hollerin', cussin', tellin' folks they got to get out of the way and screamin' "Vice Lawd" because they want everybody to know who they are. The other gang does the same thing.

Sometimes so the police wouldn't notice, small groups would go down different blocks, but if there wasn't far to go, you could call the police and they wouldn't be there for the next half-hour. By then you got a full-scale gang war.

When the two groups meet, they thump until either the man comes or they get knocked out, cut up or shot. Everybody has something to identify them. The Cobras had a big sweater with a Cobra snake on it, and the Lords had capes like Batman, an earring, and sometimes black scarves because most of the Lords had processes at that time.

During the fight, the baddest guys in the Vice Lords meet the baddest guys in the Cobras. Usually they cuff from the fists because they have the talent for boxing and the main reputation is from fighting: How many guys can he whip and how many did he dust in the gang fight?

Some guys just got downright whipped and could go home and sleep it off; others were hospitalized with wounds by knives, brass knuckles or a board with a nail in it; and some just ran off before the fight started.

The next day everybody recuperates, but fighting goes on until one group wins. There are small bodies of bad dudes with enough heart to look for the Cobras and Cobras who look for Lords. This goes on until enough folks have been caught and they stop looking for each other. It stays that way until somebody says again that the Cobras need dusting.

In 1960, Pep came back from St. Charles and found that one of his lieutenants, Possum, had turned to the Morphines. He went down and rapped to him, but Possum was headstrong. He had two to three hundred fellas and the hood was up tight. Pep learned that the Morphines had constantly been spreading animosity against the Lords so there was war against them for about six months.

"They was kind of die-hard. It took us all through the winter, snow and shit, to roll down and break them up. We brought Possum and all their leadership to the Vice Lords and gave them their rank back."

When we wanted something, we took it. When we wanted a school in the Cherokees' neighborhood, we had to take it. Cupid had come into the Lords from the Morphines and was involved in taking Herzl School. He was young, about fourteen, but he was mean and wild.

"We were getting drunk around Gregory School, and everybody say, 'Well, let's go get Herzl, man.' The Cherokees was the roughest gang on Sixteenth, so we had a meeting with some of the older fellas and our ladies and they say, 'Well, we gonna take Herzl.' That's ours.

"The next thing you know everybody was goin' to Herzl. We rolled two or three nights in a row or one or two nights a week. We rolled to show them that we could take it if we wanted it. And after we took it, we didn't want it 'cuz there wasn't nothin' happening. Then the next thing we say, 'Let's keep it 'cuz there was a lot of pretty girls goin' there and I like women — that's why my name is Cupid.' "

After Herzl the chiefs of the Lords rapped to the leaders of the Cherokees and told them they were going to be Vice Lords or they would have to leave the neighborhood. They wouldn't leave so the Lords rolled every night to take Sixteenth. Cupid was there again.

"When I say rollin', I mean fuckin' 'em up. We went to kickin' 'em in the butt, you dig?"

Some of the Cherokees joined the Cobras, some the Imperial Knights, but most got with the Lords. The Imperial Knights had Tommy Johnson, Sammy Mitchell, Fresh-Up Wade, Little Bo, and they had more members than the Vice Lords. But in another month the Lords pulled together and oiled them out. They were dusted and the whole club became Vice Lords.

The next group to handle was the Braves because they had gotten bold and were harassing some of the younger Lords. When Pep finally caught up with some Braves, the Braves' chief got a pistol on him. But Calloway was standing in a doorway and said why don't he fight Pep fair. The dude tried to fight fair, but he didn't have a win so he tried to get the gun back. By that time, Pep was around the corner. The next day he declared war.

It took about three months because the Braves lived in the projects out east, but when the Lords finished there was only one club from Pulaski all the way east to the lake, from Chicago Avenue to Cermak. The only other major club was the Egyptian Cobras on the other side of Pulaski, a club that thought they was invulnerable.

Pep went to Franklin Park and gave the Cobras an ultimatum: to change their name to Vice Lords in twenty-four hours.

They sent a message for Pep to lick outta their ass. They weren't going to change their name.

Pep gathered his troops that night and told the Cobras he was giving them a second chance and not to cross Pulaski until they gave an answer, "and it better be the right answer."

The Cobras sent another message to suck out of their ass again and Pep or none of the Vice Lords had better cross the other side of Pulaski.

This went on for about a week, then Pep decided to make an attack. The Cobras used to hang out at a show in K-Town called the Arena, so Pep stashed his troops in the park and went into the show.

"I went in the show with ten from the stronghold, and the Cobras was talkin' bullshit. So I went up to the front and walked across the screen with my cape and my cane and hat.

"One of them spotted me and say that's that jive Peppilow. So they apprehended me, and one of my lieutenants got on out and wired up my troops. About the time they got to the show, the discussion with me and the Cobras was really hot. They had me uptight; the only thing that kept me whoofin' at 'em and standin' my ground was the females kept lookin' and sayin' that's Peppilow, he ain't gonna back off nothin'. My eight lieutenants that was left was just standin' by me tryin' to make sure didn't nothin' happen to me.

"After one of my lieutenants came back and Wren was with him, I knew my troops was there, so I told the Cobras: " 'Well, this talkin' is over; I told you dudes that I don't want no more Egyptian Cobras on this West Side.'

"So the dude say, 'Fuck you, man.'

"I say, 'OK, get your troops together, man, and come on outside, 'cause if we can't get along, we gonna get it on!'

"They came outside and saw my troops across the street and they all start tryin' to split. We got to bustin' heads as long as we could keep up with them jokers."

So the humbug started. They'd fall on us and fire some of us up. We'd fall back on them and fire some of them up. Finally Pep said damn this and got the troops together to clean out K-Town. About five hundred Lords crept down Madison and Cermak to come in from Kostner on the other side. They went through the neighborhood shooting, kicking ass, and busting in the head everybody they saw.

The next day the Cobras made a counter attack. But we had infiltrated the Cobras and found out when they were coming. The Lords were waiting in apartment buildings, in gangways, and on roofs; the Cobras were moving down in a straight line on both sides of the street. Pep spotted them and the humbug broke out.

"We was around Gregory School and they didn't know where we came from. We caught one of their lieutenants and I started stabbin' him in the neck and the head. He didn't die so that next day when he came to, he put the police on me."

Pep got six months in the Bridewell, the Cook County House of Corrections, and with him out of the way, the Cobras started falling on the fellas again. Worried about Pep's leaving, the fellas weren't putting up a hard scuffle until Goat's brother, Dee Dee, was killed.

Dee Dee was sixteen, the leader of about two hundred midget Vice Lords, and the Cobras shot him with a high-powered rifle when he was going back to roll on them after they had fallen on him. He was a die-hard Vice Lord to the heart.

The fellas wired up Pep in the Bridewell and he skinned it down that the Cobras must be weak as a lamb when he got out. The war horses went out and killed about three Cobras and shot Stump Daddy's brother, Popeye. Hershey Foster got a concussion, and Leroy Brown, another leader, was caught and stabbed about forty-two times.

There was fighting every day. They would come past Pulaski and try to shoot at us and duck back over and then we would go back and catch five or ten of them. Anybody in K-Town had to be a Cobra so it didn't make any difference if we knew them or not; we kicked their ass.

When Pep came home the Cobras were cool, but the Imperials were trying to come back so Pep took the fellas to an Imperial dance at the YMCA.

"We just tore up the whole Y — broke windows, caused about fifty thousand dollars' damage to the building. The Y put out a warrant on me so I know the man was lookin' for me. I went out to Franklin Park and tore that up, and the Cobras had a poolroom and we turned over the tables and burnt them and shit and broke up the restaurant where they hung out."

When Pep was busted, there was no good evidence against him, but the judge had made up his mind and said he was going to cut off the head and the body would die. He gave Pep a year in the House of Corrections.

The Bridewell

With so much gangbanging, the Lords kept the jails in business. By the end of two or three years of gangfighting, most of the Lords had been locked up at some time or another. A lot of guys spent as much time in jail as on the street. If you were under seventeen the judge doesn't give you time but recommends IYC, the Illinois Youth Commission, and you make your own time. The ones who didn't go cutting and really stomping went to the Audy Home and the others were sent to the diagnostic center in Joliet, Illinois. In the diagnostic center they determine where to send you and that depends on the crime, your past record, and how you behave at Joliet. They may send you to St. Charles, Sheridan, or one of the camps.

If you're over seventeen they can send you to the County Jail, the House of Corrections, or the penitentiary. The most you can do in the County and the House of Corrections is eighteen months, and anything over that, you have to serve in the penitentiary. If you get under a year the judge can send you anyplace he wants to, and if you get over two years the Joliet Diagnostic Center determines if you go to the Pontiac, Joliet, or Stateville penitentiary. For less than a year and a day, the judge could also send you to Vandalia, which is a farm where the inmates grow everything they eat. A lot of fellas didn't want to go to Vandalia because there was a lot of prejudice since most of the guards were Southerners, and they say Stateville was a cruel place, so they would go to Pontiac if they could.

Most of the fellas that got caught knew how much time they would get before going to court. You never carried something you couldn't pay for and there wasn't any thinking about the fellas getting you out on bond. If your mama didn't get you out, as Toehold says, "You was stuck in that motherfucker." After Toe's mother got him out once or twice, "She told me I ain't gonna spend no more money tryin' to get

24

you out of jail. Get your own self out or do the time. I never did ask her. When the judge gave me a year, I do nine months and eight days and get on out.

Going to jail was like starting in a new world. You never get conditioned in jail, but you more or less adjust to your case. Most of your dreams are about beating the case and seeing yourself back on the street. As Charley found out, ''It scared the shit out of me . . . grew gray hairs around my nuts, knowin' I was goin' to trial.''

When you go to jail anything can happen to you whether you're guilty or not guilty. You don't know what's going on and there are guards dogging you all day.

Pete feels that ''you got to do what they say or go to the hole. It's a motherfucker up there. When whitey ain't on your back, it's a nigger that think white. He gonna tell you what to do, how to go to bed, how to make your bed, how to eat. Your beliefs don't mean shit to them, and a weakling ain't got a chance.''

There's homosexuality in jails but more in the prisons, where guys have longer time to serve than in the County or the Bridewell. One inmate from the County says, ''You find a punk at the County Jail and he's everybody's woman on three tiers. You didn't need but five sissies and you got the whole place uptight.''

As he explains, ''Guys doin' the fuckin' inside may not do it outside. Now, the one that will do it inside and outside, he's a freak too. He don't give a fuck where he's at. Most of the cats in there play with themselves, but in jail they look at this as normal. If you don't beat your meat, then somethin' else wrong with you. You must be fucked up or queer anyway. Society looks at that from the outside, but if you ain't went through the goddamn thing, you don't really get the full meaning.''

A lot of young cats go in and the jail makes them into criminals, so when they come out they don't care if they go back. Some are even happier in jail than out. A cat can eat three times a day, rest in the evening and not think about women. He goes to school, gets his radio in the cell, reads his paper, and he hasn't got a problem in the world. He lays dead.

Although there is brutality in the jail and the only thing some people learn is to avoid the guards, being locked up never stopped the Lords. Jail was accepted as something like the street. You could do almost everything in there that you could do outside. Jail was just another experience.

Many members were recruited from the jails. Calloway was arrested for thirty days, sixty days, ninety days, sometimes six months, but usually for short periods, and he was steady getting members who stayed together when they came out; and Pep boasted that "no matter what most of the dudes was when they came in, when they came out they was Lords." Even if a dude didn't change gangs, when you spend a year in jail together, you become friends. You've got something in common; you live the same life, you have the same philosophy. When you get out of jail and you see the same guy you did that year with, you don't want to kill him, although the law in the gang says you gotta whip him, so you whip him a little to let him know he's in the wrong neighborhood. Toehold knows the time "we used to get drunk with a cat and then say we gotta whip your ass anyway."

Pep was seventeen when he went to the Bridewell in 1960. He spent a week in isolation in the youth unit, and when he came out he could see that the older dudes were in control. He layed there to find out who was who until one day he just started knocking people out and got sent to the hole. He finished his six months, stayed out two weeks, and got sent back for a year. This time they wouldn't let him in the youth unit and he was too young to go in the men's dorm so they put him in the hole. The warden didn't know what to do with him. He was a threat in the youth unit, where he had started a riot, so finally they decided that maybe some of the older men could handle him in the men's dorm.

"The first week I layed cool. I knew a dude that used to box and he started tellin' the old dudes that I was a helluva young dude. They put me in the kitchen and one day while I was serving food, some bad dude came through the line. I was just givin' out one porkchop a man, so he came up and say:

"'Say man, you don't know where you at—I gets two.'

"He called me a young punk, and the four or five dudes that I was regular with told me to ease up 'cuz that dude is treacherous. The dude was talkin' about what he would do; he was gonna fuck me up if I didn't give him another pork chop—so I told the man:

"'Dig, I ain't gonna give ya nothin' but one and I don't think you gonna do nothin' to me.'

"So one word led to another and he told me after chow time that he wants to see me in the day room. He went back to his table and Tony told me not to meet with the dude. Glenn told me to be cool and that there was about ten to fifteen of them. They was dopefiends and hustlers from out south on Forty-seventh Street.

"So I was givin' out coffee and I told the dude, forget it, you know, you can have a porkchop. So he was whoofin' in front of his fellas and say:

"'No, I'm gonna fuck you, young motherfucker.'"

"I went back and got me a pitcher of hot coffee and when he came back I just poured it down his head. He jumped up and then I oiled him. When I oiled him right there in the place, all the dudes was shocked to see a seventeen-, eighteen-year-old dude handle this other dude like this.

"The next day he came back still weak and wanted some more, so I just took this big paddle that you stir up oatmeal with and commenced to operatin' with that paddle and busted his skull.

"They put the dude in the hospital the next day, but about a week later he wanted some more, so I just went with him head up and oiled the dude completely with my fists.

"Everybody started talkin' about it 'cuz he was supposed to be the big dude around there. My name started ringin' and I told Tony that I'm not givin' out no more food. Tony took over as captain of the kitchen and I started sittin' in the back.

"Then I told all the dudes that stayed with me that I didn't want them givin' out none of the food, so they just stayed around me and kept clean and we hired some dudes to give out the food. I put one of them in the laundry to check that out and see who was runnin' the place. I sent an ultimatum and told them what I wanted and how I wanted it done. We had the kitchen already and I ambushed two of the clerks and let them know which way things was goin' and they fell in line.

"After three months of my year, almost damn near the whole institution was under one thumb. It wasn't that I could whip 'em all; they knew if they didn't stay in line they would wake up falling off one of them galleries.

"Eventually we took care of any Lord that came in. They ate the best, they wore the best, and they slept in the best places. Any dude on the street that was a Lord knew when he was busted that he would be well taken care of when he went in the place, so being locked up was no threat for the Lords. It didn't matter if they got locked up or not.

"As dudes came in, they saw it was profitable to be a Vice Lord. Even Cobras turned into Lords."

When the city found out what was going on, Pep was sent to isolation for thirty days. When he got out they put him in the west cell house, a prison slum.

"You have to shit in a bucket and empty it in the morning. I stayed there for about a week and then sent word that I wanted out.''

When Captain C of the Bridewell went on vacation, Glenn processed Pep's hair as a disguise and for three months a white lieutenant saw Pep every day but didn't recognize him until it was time for Pep to go home.

Glenn and a few others — Ball, Chuck, and Flukie — got out before Pep, and Glenn helped to tighten up the set. He had come in as a dopefiend, but when he came out he was a stone Lord to the bone. When his name started to grow they started calling him Sugarcane because he was tall and slender and the girls figured he was a sugar cane. Nicknames were used to make it difficult for the police to catch up with the fellas, but eventually most of the police knew the real names because most of the fellas had been locked up so many times.

Once a week someone would visit Pep, and Tommy Lee, who was in charge while Pep was away, would write. During the visit, Pep let the Lords know how he wanted things done, what to do, and when to do it.

Organization secrets were discovered from Cobras, Imperials, Braves, Night Owls, and others who went into the Bridewell. We found out where they hid weapons, where so and so lived, and who was the leadership. This information was piped out since the Lords had a semi-intelligence agency within the Bridewell and within the penitentiary. Word gets around fast in jail; you can't hide anything. One dude might be working in the kitchen and you happen to go to the kitchen. You get to rapping about things that happen on your tier and his tier and the word just spreads.

You can also use the toilet to pass information by pushing the button and hollering down through the toilet to talk to the man on the next tier. Or you could call through the air vent over the toilet. The guards can hear you, but after everybody is locked up, the guards go outside or down to the front office. If you're in cell 37 on E-4, you can talk to the guy in 37 on E-3.

In the Bridewell, nurses, guards, social workers, preachers and inmates going home were used for communications. If someone was going home he was programmed to remember certain facts and we would write numbers on his back. They usually strip an inmate when he goes out, but they just search his clothes. The guards, social workers, and others cooperated not so much because there was something in it for them but because they lived in the community and saw the Lords every day and night. For the safety of them and the family, they would cooperate.

Lords Run It

Sugarcane expanded the empire in 1961. When Pep got out nobody had to sleep on the street and there were no wants.

If it snowed and the fellas didn't want to go outside, Pep might get in the car and find ten or twenty girls to keep the fellas happy. Most of the fellas never had to pay for getting their hair done because Glenn had set up a process shop, and Pep went with a girl whose aunt owned a clothing store and she ordered clothes from a discount store, so everybody kept clean. In a sense we had our own welfare system.

Pep could keep two to three hundred dollars in his pocket by this time, but most of his money would go to his lieutenants and on down the chain of command. There were a million different ways to get money. Nothing was safe on the streets. We would get money from liquor stores, liquor salesmen, clothing stores, dudes off the street, dope peddlers, reefer peddlers, pill pushers, barbecue places, stickups, boosters—any way we could get it. Boosting was when the girls would go in stores and steal clothes and we would sell them on the streets for discount prices or give them away if somebody was mellow or we wanted to keep a family uptight.

We grew and grew and people heard about us throughout the city as the word got out that the Lords were putting pressure on the syndicate. Dudes who wanted to open a tavern on the West Side would find Pep or one of his lieutenants and ask about opening.

We had a closely knit brotherhood and we had isolated all the gangs. Things were going fine until October 1961, when Glenn, some other Vice Lords and a Vice Lady were down in the basement on Millard after a big haul which split eighteen hundred dollars among four chiefs. While they were down there, somebody knocked and Glenn opened the door. When he did his heart was blown out. He was dead.

Some people believe the syndicate hit Glenn, but more than likely they were after Pep because we'd been out for protection, and the syndicate did run the area.

The police came in, ransacked the crib, found about six automatics, twelve pistols, shotguns, and two .30-30s with scopes. They assumed that no one from outside the Lords could have got within the neighborhood, killed a high-ranking Lord, and got out, so they locked up Pep and his brother for about seventy-two hours.

CHICAGO DAILY NEWS, October 3, 1961
VICE LORD MEMBER SHOT DOWN

Glenn Miles, 21, said by police to be a member of the Senior Vice Lords youth gang, was shot to death early Tuesday when he went to answer a knock at a door.

Miles was shot twice in the chest with a shotgun that was fired through the glass of the door of a basement apartment in which he was living at 2135 5. Millard.

The landlord, Robert Jones, called police.

Det. W. Boderson said Miles' roommate, Edward Perry, 22, whom he identified as president of the Senior Vice Lords, said he believes the shotgun blasts were meant for him (Perry).

Perry told police the shooting was in retaliation for a fight the Vice Lords had with another gang several weeks ago.

Miles, who lived with two other Vice Lord members, was alone when the shooting occurred.

The night after Glenn died, all the Lords got together and began to roll on every club that might have had anything to do with the shooting. We rolled every night for about a month, just shooting and busting heads. Anybody we caught that we thought had done it, we would try to cut his tongue out, but nothing came up and the police still insisted that the Lords probably had done it.

After two months of thinking about Glenn's murder, a lot of us got scared and lost interest in building up a syndicate. Lords now nineteen and twenty had gone to jail and become aware that life was more precious than what they thought when they were fifteen and sixteen and what seemed to be fun shook the ones that lived because a dude gets to wondering how in hell did he get away without being maimed or killed.

We started hanging around, slowly deteriorating. We were hanging around by the hundreds — going to parties, humbugging every now and then — but most of the older Lords started going home at night. We even went to lounges and taverns, something we normally wouldn't do. We drank heavy and we could get it free, so there wasn't any problem about waking up the next morning with a headache. In 1962 and 1963 most of us were half drunk all the time. Some were working so on weekends we would find a place to humbug.

One of the humbugs was with the Roman Saints, a group that came up when the Lords were looking west at the Cobras. Eugene Brown, who had been a Lord, started the Saints and stayed around the Central Park Theater, which used to belong to the Imperials. The Lords didn't pay much attention because we went downtown to the movies after the ladies stopped going to the Central Park.

Most of the fights were around Hess School where the Roman Queens jumped on the younger girls to get them to tell where the older Vice Ladies were hanging.

Each gang had a female division; there were the Vice Ladies, the Cobraettes, the Imperialettes, and the Roman Queens. The Vice Ladies had girls like Cupid's sister, Foot, a gangfighter and razor packer; Mary Wolfe — sort of tall, real thin, wore pants all the time and a scarf around her hair and loved to start somethin'; Cherry, who was president and a little bit worse than the others; and Marcia Ann, Ernestine, Big Shirley, and Dini.

A Vice Lady was there for whatever was needed. Whatever the assignment, a Vice Lady would go all out. If she had to go with a cat, "you not gonna go with a cat and not fuck him, and for her to get in where they at, she got to go through these changes. Quite naturally, we fucked them too."

A Vice Lady was also used for carrying guns. The police couldn't search females so she could carry a shotgun up under her dress and the fellas could walk alongside. Today there are cars and you put a gun in a car and hide it until you get to where a guy is; then you take it out and shoot the shit out of him. Back then everybody walked and if a cop would stop and shake the guys down and a broad has the piece, the fellas fronted until she got away.

At one time the Vice Ladies gangbanged as much as the fellas and whoever was going with them had to be a thumper too. They used to carry chains in their brassieres — chains, razors, anything they could get up in there. You couldn't slap 'em and walk away; you had to sure 'nough get down.

When the Roman Queens jumped on younger girls, Vice Ladies like Dini went around to where they were.

"We wanted to know why they got jumped on and they couldn't tell us nothin' so we just started battlin'. We went from fist to fist, or else chains, bottles, and bricks."

Most of the time just the girls fought, but sometimes the fellas would jump in. If the Roman Saints helped the Roman Queens, then the Lords helped the Ladies. Sometimes though, the Vice Ladies would actually jump in to fight the boys.

The Roman Saints didn't take long to dust and one Saint had a simple explanation: "We just went into the thing and we got dusted. Seems like as soon as we hurt one of their fellas, they come back five or six strong. We never did get a chance to meet just one."

When the Saints were getting dusted, they united with the Cobras in one fight, but they still lost. Just like countries going to war. You unite to save your country, or territory, and this is what the Roman Saints tried to do.

The Cobras were different. The turf was too big and there were too many members. There was no way of getting control. We couldn't get them and they couldn't get us. Cats were getting dusted, getting time, and getting shot, so we just said Pulaski is the dividing line. This was like Russia fighting America. Why fight Russia when they got as much stuff as we got?

In 1964, Eugene Hairston, Calloway's cousin, kicked off the Blackstone Rangers on the South Side and some of the Lords would go out south because they wouldn't get busted. For about a year and a half we used to go out there two or three times a week and help any way we could. When they first started, they were the Blackstone Raiders, and about 1965 they became the Rangers.

If we can help them now, we still help, but after they got themselves together, our traveling slacked off. Sixteenth and Lawndale became the stronghold because there were Lords there every day, every night, and if you got in some trouble, all you had to do was go around there. That year all the branches that used to travel started to stay where they lived and instead of everybody being just Vice Lords, a lot of names started: Ugly Frank started the Traveller Vice Lords; Billy Washington got the Congress Vice Lords; Cupid, Dino, Bolock, and Shane formed the War Lords; and the dudes around Sixteenth formed the Renegades and City Vice Lords.

There were the Kedzie, Albany, and Terrible Vice Lords (KAT), the Cermak Vice Lords, the Conservative Village Vice Lords on Pulaski, the 7-Crown Syndicate Vice Lords in K-Town, the Cicero Vice Lords,

Independence Vice Lords, Lake St. Vice Lords, Madison Vice Lords, and Chocolate Corner Vice Lords.

There were also the Ambrose Vice Lords, the Black Orpheus Vice Lords, Spanish Vice Lords, Insane Vice Lords, the Enforcers, the Invisible Vice Lords, and the Unknown Vice Lords.

There were at least twenty-six branches and eight to ten thousand Lords. Together they made the Vice Lord Nation.

They had their own sets, their own parties, their own girls, their own dudes that told them what to do. The members didn't come into contact with each other the way we used to because the club was so big, but in their hearts everybody was Lord and Peppilow came to be Chief of the Nation of Lords.

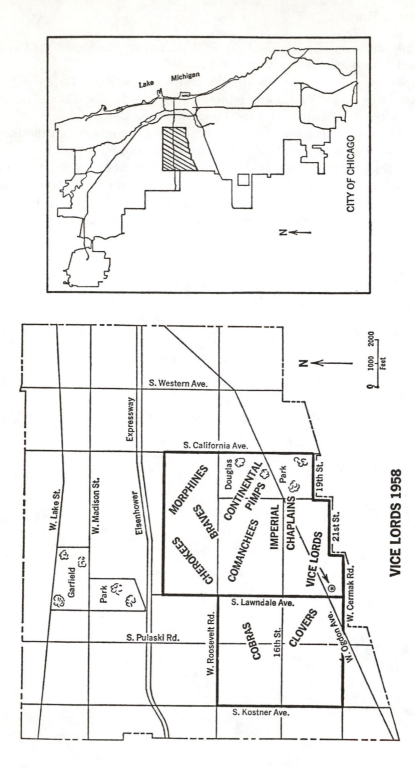

CITY OF CHICAGO

VICE LORDS 1958

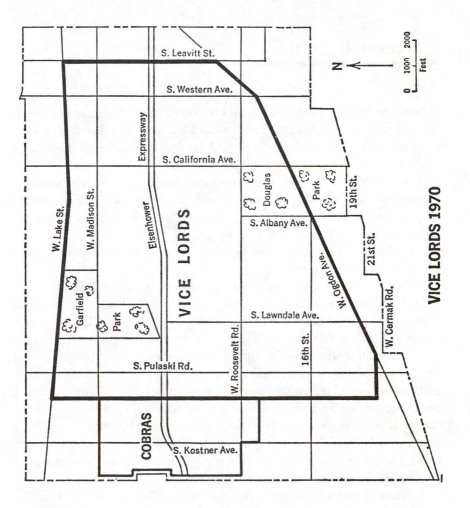

VICE LORDS 1970

Wherever It Go Down

When Lords were gangbanging, there were always fights and parties. If another club gave a party, Lords would go there and tear it up — kick out the windows, take the records and mayonnaise jar with the hole in the top that you throw your quarters and dimes into, and whip the girls and the guys because they were not Lords or Ladies. If Lords gave a party somebody would come that nobody knew or another gang would fall in to tear it up and we'd end up running them back home, although sometimes they tore up and ran us.

Cupid can't remember a party since he was thirteen and fourteen where there wasn't a fight.

"Usually I'd be one of the dudes that started the fight. I had my own little clique and we'd start the fight and then let the bigger fellows take over. We'd always start it with somebody big and the fellas wouldn't let them hurt us so that would pull in everybody.

"I was full of wine and fighting was something to do. It was fun 'til I went to gettin' cut and gettin' whipped. Then I learned some sense and I went to tightenin' up. But it was too late; I had gone too far. I had a reputation and people knew me, so wherever I was most of the time I had to fight. Usually I would have somebody with me, but sometimes I'd get drunk and just go down and start a big gang fight and I knew I couldn't whip all of them. There'd be six or seven guys on a corner in another gang and I'd go down there and start hittin' on 'em. They'd end up whippin' me and runnin' me back and I would tell the other fellas and they'd get together to go back and get the whole club.

"I should have been dead a long time ago, but I believe that I ain't gonna die 'til my time comes, and I'm gonna keep fighting for the Lords 'til my time does come."

When he was sixteen, Cupid liked the Lords' parties because this was a chance to get action with the ladies.

"One of the fella's mother would let him give a quarter party or birthday party in the basement. The party would start about eight but usually don't nobody come until about ten, maybe eleven. That's when it starts to jumpin'. Like they say, the nighttime is the right time.

"So it starts jumpin' about eleven and that's when you can do anything you want. Since the party is in a basement, you can go in there, get a coupla drinks and start to do your thing. You might see a girl you be wantin' for a long time so this is your chance. You show her you got a little dough, some reefer — you real hip, you know — and you and her ease on off. Usually there are three or four rooms in a basement, sometimes five and six, but a lot of times you have to stand in line to get any room. Nobody lives there and the rooms are usually just for storage. In some buildings they have washing machines and dryers so we'll go down there and if people got clothes on the line, we spread them on the floor and use that. If there ain't nothin' down there, we use our coat. If it's hot and there ain't no coat, we just get on the floor and you don't need nothin'.

"If you're married or livin' with somebody and you sneak off at the party, you're not supposed to let her know. That's called creepin'. You make a quick creep. Usually it don't take no more than ten or fifteen minutes to get your nuts off so you tell her you went to the store. She be up there dancin' or somethin', so either you cut out or the girl cuts out and the other one follows. You be done planned this with the girl earlier.

"When you get to the party you go to hittin' on the girl. She be in one room, your wife in another, and you sneak in there and whisper to her and get her high. But you keep lettin' your wife see you so she don't get suspicious. Then you tell the broad to meet you downstairs: you got some more reefer and you gonna bring down a coupla jugs. So she be goin' downstairs and you tell your old lady you be right back.

Cupid was married before he was twenty and his wife had caught him in some awkward positions once or twice:

"Like I went over to one of her girlfriend's house and there was another girl there. The other girlfriend had gone to the store and she left this girl to keep the house. I figure I can go on and get this here, so me and her go on the bed. I was pretty high so I just forgot about lockin' the door.

"By my old lady and this other girl bein' so tight, they usually don't knock if the door is open. My old lady came in and was walkin' through the house. I thought it was this other girl, her girlfriend, until I heard her call. I say, God, that's my old lady, but by the time I get up, she come in the door and that was all.

"She ran the girl out and while she and this girl was fightin', I put on my clothes and cut out. Later on, I see the girl runnin' down the street and my old lady behind her, so I got my hat and disappeared too. I stayed away a day and when I came home, I sassed her, told her I got busted in jail, and that's why I didn't come home. We talked about what had happened and I told her it ain't gonna happen no more. She knows I mess around; she just don't want to catch me and it's not that you get tired of your wife — but you can just see somethin' you want and you try your best to get it. When you get it, there ain't nothin' to it.

"But she can't do what you do. If we go to a party I don't mind my wife dancin' and carryin' on, but she can't go in no room by herself with nobody. When it's me and her together, we don't split up unlessin' I go somewhere. I can do it but she can't; it's the man's way, his animal instinct. That's the way I feel. Like you can have a girlfriend and you can be goin' with all her partners, but she can't mess with nobody else. I feel by me bein' with this girl, I'm helpin' her; she ain't helpin' me. When you takin' a woman some money, you don't want her messin' with nobody else or givin' your money to some other guy. She gonna do what I tell her or me and her gonna split up, or maybe I'll bust her head.

"Women get it in their heads that they can tell you what to do, what not to do; tell you when you can come home and when you can't. Then when you don't do what they say, they want to divorce you, put the police on you, or have you give 'em alimony. Don't nobody want to hear that; that's just like bein' in jail. Most other guys I know feel the same way."

In one way or another, there have been many problems because of ladies. On the street there were guys who would pat them on the ass; they wouldn't rape them, but they would squeeze their ass. She would tell her old man and as Toehold says:

"Her old man be damn fool enough to come back and get fucked up just because some cat got a handful of ass. Some guys have come back out and caught the dudes and busted their heads, but some of them couldn't get away.

"If it had been me and my wife come home and tell me that a bunch of guys down there felt her ass and called her a bunch of bitches, quite naturally I'm gonna get up and come out, but if all the women went and told their husband or old man that some of these guys down here have squeezed their ass, there probably would be a lot more dead. A lot of women just didn't say anything — not that they liked the idea; they just thought before they got home. They know if he comes down here, he might kill somebody or get killed.''

Actually we were just looking for something to do because we didn't have any reason to keep out of trouble. All we could do was just drink scrap iron, smoke reefers, and look for a humbug. There was nothing to occupy our minds.

At that time, there were only gangs and blood. Blood was white port wine and Kool-Aid. You took a bottle of white port, mixed it with strawberry Kool-Aid, and you had blood. When one of the fellas got killed, Pep suggested that the first drink always be for the fellas that's dead, so the first drink is always poured on the sidewalk. Some pour a "CVL," but the main thing is just to pour the first drink.

Everybody in the gang drank wine and very few used drugs. If you were a dopey, you were all right, but you had no time for the gang. You had to hustle money for drugs; you didn't have time to go to house parties, beaches or gangbangs, and then you weren't a regular.

Winos get high and fight, but a dopey gets high, goes to sleep and hasn't got time for humbugging. Some have died from an overdose and some have gone to Lexington, Kentucky, to kick, but there is very little the organization can do once a cat is out on his own. You seldom find one in a gang and you seldom find a gang that's got dopeys.

Marijuana was different. Anybody that's smoking marijuana doesn't get in trouble. He thinks different. If something is too loud he stays more alert. He doesn't want to be around something loud so no one can ease up on him. And a cat couldn't provoke him to fight if he's smoking marijuana because he thinks faster. He might say, ''Now why should I fool with this square ass sonofabitch: 'Fuck ya, man, I'm gone.' ''

But when you're drinking that alcohol, you think you can whip twenty people and you might not whip even one. Some guys would drink four to five pints a day, every day, and all that alcohol makes them do things they never dreamed of doing. You get that courage. The alcohol makes you think you can do more and that's what a person needs when he goes to fight. The Indians would get crazy high before they go and attack; and if there was a humbug most of the Lords got high before rolling. You didn't become a better fighter, but you're faster with the alcohol. You might chop a cat's head off with that alcohol, but if you go fight him sober, you might hit him with one punch and the cat is laying down and you couldn't even kick him any more. If you're full of alcohol you can stomp him all day long and think nothing of it.

Sometimes a group of Lords went to the North Side drinking and if we saw four or five guys who didn't look right, we just got out and started something with them. It didn't matter if they were a gang or not. They might be sitting down with some young ladies and we know if we start talking to their ladies, that's a fight. When one of them says something to us, that's our reason to start.

We have jumped on quite a few white guys just because we didn't like them; when we see them, we just jump out and fuck over them. We have gone so far as just to mess with some of the people in the neighborhood, the people we see every day. They just happen to walk up and catch us in one of those moods, and one of the fellas runs up, slaps him down and kicks him. We laughed.

But all the fellas didn't do this, and everyone didn't have the same attitude about fighting. Some dudes like to gang up on a cat; others like to stand and meet head up. For Toehold a fight was nice "when you gotta dude that will fight back."

"A cat, you hit him once or twice and he cover up, that ain't nothin'. I don't jump on nobody like that. But a cat that fights back, I dig that. Any time you could fight nice, cats were going to say, 'Damn, that cat can sure 'nuf get down.'"

Toehold hated to see ten or fifteen dudes jump on one.

"If anybody jump on my friends, I'm gonna jump on them; like if a fella be goin' home and them dudes have thirty or forty people and they bloody him up and knock a hole in his head with chains and bricks and look for us to accept that. We wasn't gonna accept that shit.

"If anybody mess with me, I don't say nothin'. I wait 'til I get the play. I always felt that my day gonna come. He got me now, but he ain't gonna sleep with you. So I get the drop on him, and where he might have let me go, I ain't gonna let him go. That was his fault for lettin' me go . . . it ain't mine.

"When the man got an advantage over you, why you wantta lay and talk shit and get killed? That don't make sense. Just go on and tell him everything is mellow, brother, and just cut on out. Later, he might buy you a drink and you buy him a drink — sweeten him up and say, 'Man, you know I can't do nothin' to you.' Next thing you know, half his head be broke in.

"A lotta people call it stealin', but that's usin' your head. A cat know he done got into it, he ain't supposed to turn his head. A lot of people

CHICAGO SUN-TIMES—August 19, 1961
13 TEENS FACE GRAND JURY IN
FATAL BEATING

A coroner's jury sat in a sweltering morgue inquest room Friday and heard testimony that a man was killed after he was asked for 10 cents.

After the hearing, the jury recommended that 13 members of the Midget Vice Lords gang be held to the grand jury on the charge of murdering Chrispulo Mangaser, 56, of 1811 S. Lawndale.

One of the gang members, Chester (The Fool) Soloman, 17, testified that he approached Mangaser on the night of Aug. 11 and said, 'Mister, could I have a dime?

I Hit Him'

"He said to me, 'What do you think I am, your daddy?' and when he said that I hit him—with my left hand, Soloman said.

Mangaser fell to the pavement, striking his head, other testimony revealed, and then "about 14 other" Vice Lords descended upon him.

"They beat him up and hit him with an umbrella, it looked like," said a witness, Milton Foley, of 1918 S. Lawndale.

Foley said the youths had been lingering across the street from the scene of the beating at 1903 S. Lawndale, before the first boy hit Mangaser.

Rip Victims Pockets

Mangaser's trousers were nearly torn from his body. Gang members testified they ripped his pockets in search of money.

When the assailants fled Foley called police. Mangaser died last Saturday in Mount Sinai Hospital of skull and brain injuries.

After robbing Mangaser, gang members testified, they went to a restaurant and ate hamburgers and pop purchased with the $3.85 they took from the fatally injured man.

Alfred Johnson, 15, of 1412 S. Drake, known as "The Brain," recounted the attack.

Seek Rival Gang

He said the group had been to a dance in Garfield Park and then had walked to the corner of 16th and Lawndale.

"We was just hanging around laughing and joking . . . all right . . . and we got the word there was some Cobras (a rival gang) . . . all right . . . and we went looking for them (to have a fight—the Cobras had beaten up a Vice Lord named Cook Breeze)."

After failing to find the Cobras, Johnson said he broke up a fight between gang member Joseph (Crazy Joe) Shelton, 15, of 1859 S. Sawyer, and an unidentified man.

"Then the Fool (Soloman) say, 'I'm going to get some money,' Johnson said, "I didn't pay any attention . . . all right . . . The Fool hit the man, all right. An his head hit the ground—hard, all right; I heard it across the street.

"And they tore the man's pockets . . . all right. And The Fool picked up the money, and I snatched the money from him.

"I got $3.85 from him and gave $1.50 to The Fool.

Denies Seeing Beating

"I didn't see anybody kick or stomp the man. They all just went through his pockets."

Johnson said he and Soloman split the money because "the others didn't know anything about it."

Coroner Andrew J. Toman asked Johnson:

"What was your reason in going in to see the Cobras?"

"We was going to fight them."

"For what?"

Angry at Cobras

"Just to fight them, that's all."

Johnson added that he had been beaten by the Cobras some nine months ago, which, in addition to the beating of "Cool

Breeze,'' had made him angry.

"Did you report it to the police when you were beaten?" Toman asked.

"No," Johnson replied.

"Why?" Toman persisted.

"I didn't want to, that's why," said Johnson.

Tyrone Howard, 16, of 3510 W. 15th, identified as the president of the Midget Vice Lords, said the group had been drinking the night of the attack.

Tells of Drinking

He said they consumed "two quarts of beer and a quart of gin" they purchased through an unknown adult.

Mangaser's sister-in-law, Mrs. Vivian Gascon of Los Angeles, brought his battered clothing to show the jury.

She glared at the youths at the inquest.

"I hope somebody cries over you when you die like they cried over him," she said. "If I had my way I'd get rid of you like

a bunch of mad dogs — that's what you are."

Held in addition to Soloman, Johnson and Howard, was Larry (Nat) Richardson, accused of slugging Mangaser with an umbrella.

Youth Offers Alibi

Another gang member arrested for the fatal beating, John (Ringo) Chew, 17, of 1619 S. Harding, denied participation in the attack and his story was confirmed by the others.

Although he had been with the others earlier, he went home before the assault, Chew declared. Another youth, known only as "Rico," took part in the beating, the others said. Chew was arrested because of the confusion between his nickname, "Ringo" and the other boy's name.

Chew will be released if investigation proves his alibi true.

get killed like that. They jump on a man for nothin' and walk down the street braggin'. He walk about two or three steps goin' home and gets dusted goin' past one of those alleyways.''

Since a fight could happen anywhere or you could be jumped anywhere, most guys traveled around in pairs or groups. Wherever it go down, that's where it be at.

Toehold always traveled with Jim Miller and they would walk right down the street and ask another club what was happening. Both could box and neither would run off and leave the other.

"We had just bust five or six of 'em, but all they say is, 'Ain't nothin' to it, baby.' Once you put some hurtin' on somebody good, they don't much want no more trouble as long as you don't just force 'em into it. I never did just force 'em into it; I wait 'til they do somethin' to one of my friends; then I go and handle 'em.''

We didn't enjoy getting hurt but fighting was fun, and even if a fella did get hurt, he had something to identify with the rest of the fellas. Any time a guy got hurt or went to jail, he got a bit more prestige.

Cupid built his reputation in institutions as much as on the street. He was supposed to be a bad boy, so they had him in the Montefiore School in Jewtown. Montefiore was just like a regular school except that it was for people who are supposed to be hard core. If you had never been there, it scared you because the next step is jail. When Cupid was caught robbing, the next step for him was the IYC and the Joliet Diagnostic Center.

"I stayed there about a month and they was gonna let me come home, but about a week before I was supposed to go, me and the gym teacher got into it and I hit him across the head with the bar that you lift weights with. The next day they shipped me out to Sheridan and I stayed in there for eighteen months. When I came home, I did the same thing and eventually that led from IYC to the County Jail to the Bridewell.

"When you come home, people look up to you. You go to the Audy Home, stay a month, and everybody say you're a bad dude, you can take it. At Sheridan, I was on the boxing team and brought home trophies, so the fellas just started lookin' up to me and I started takin' on a leadership role."

In the gangbanging days they were saying if a guy wore a scar, he was a terrible sonofabitch, a bad dude. Later we found out that he wasn't the bad guy; the bad guy was the one who gave him the scars and bullet wounds.

Most guys didn't enjoy hurting people, but for some there was prestige in that too. Guys got a kick out of coming back and talking about what they had done to a particular person.

"Did you see me when I hit him in his eye?"

"Yeah, but I'm the one that cut him."

" — and I crowned him with the baseball bat."

This was to make sure that everyone knew that he had been part of the humbug. Then he wouldn't be labeled as a cat that didn't participate in the fights.

Guns came in the picture late because many gunfighters understood that gang fights were to prove your manhood. Gang fights were not for killing, and most of the time they were hand to hand. Guns came in with cats that couldn't fight and then everybody had to get a gun.

The first weapons were bricks, pop bottles, stones and sticks. Then came the switchblade knives. The shotguns and pistols came later in the sixties and this brought most of the killings.

At that time we used radio aerials to make zip guns because they would fit a .22. You wrapped it with a wooden frame, rubber band, a spring and a nail and BANG! You can also stick an antenna in the barrel of a toy snub-nose .38, sharpen the hammer, and BANG again!

Zip guns got obsolete because you had a lot of misfirings, but then cats went all the way for the real jive, the real gun. You couldn't buy them so you had to find other ways. There were a lot lying around and everybody knew that a guy in the store kept a gun for protection, so you run into the store and say put your hands up.

Another place was the police, and Goat used to jump on their scooters and snatch their guns. "At that time, all you got was sixty days at St. Charles, and 80 percent of the gang would volunteer to go to the farm for a week or sixty days to get a gun. When you gotta gun, you is a bad cat. So a guy would steal a cop's Magnum, hide it, go to St. Charles, come back, and he had a Magnum. You didn't tell him nothin' 'cause he had a Magnum and you didn't. He had six bullets and if he was lucky enough to get the whole thing, he had twelve. You didn't tell him shit.

"The police were cool too because they had to ride in that fuckin' scooter and not know who was gonna dust 'em next. Before society knew it, gangs had more guns than the army. Guys that wanted to take over started shooting, and as TV became more adventurous, guns became even more popular. Guys got help from Elliot Ness, Al Capone, and the Purple Gang. A cat thought why should he rassle with a dude when he can saw off a rifle and dust two or three. Why take fifty guys when you can take a sawed-off shotgun and wipe out the group. But even in watching movies or television, everybody was smart enough to know what he could use and what the hell he couldn't use. Nobody ever said we want a tommy-gun. Now the shotgun, that's us. We could use that."

Then cats came up with the idea of gas bombs. They came in the early 1960s when molotov cocktails were thrown into dance parties. One Lord who at the time was a Van Dyke remembers a party where the Braves broke out the windows and threw in molotov cocktails. The bomb exploded, everybody caught on fire, and the Braves waited outside for the people on fire. Then they jumped on them and beat them.

The Lords used molotov cocktails once against the Cobras when we were around Gregory School. We drew them into a box canyon, cut them off and started throwing gas bombs on them from the roof. They stopped coming, but generally gas bombs were not good for streetfighting because the cats would throw them in the streets and everybody would scatter. They went slowly out of existence because they were too much bother.

Another idea from television and the movies was the burial car, like in "The Untouchables." A dude would go out and steal a black Cadillac and everybody in the car was an assassin. They used to ride around in the black Cadillac and shoot at other gangs. Or we would take shotguns and tie handkerchiefs around the barrels of them like the Indians used

CHICAGO DAILY NEWS, November 10, 1961
HOPE FLICKERS ANEW FOR
MAIMED COP

All the News Isn't Bad
For Sgt. Burns, Who Lost Eye

BY EDMUND J. ROONEY

Worry creased the brow of Police Sgt. Joseph J. Burns, 53, Chicago's latest police hero.

"I hope my bosses won't make me quit now that I only have one eye," he said.

"But, what can a one-eyed policeman do? I've loved the job. It's tough to think that it might be all over now . . ."

* * *

SURGEONS at Presbyterian — St. Luke's Hospital removed Burns' left eye this week after Burns, on duty, was stamped upon and beaten by a gang of 35 young toughs Oct. 21.

Burns of 6123 S. Whipple, a stocky six-footer, was assaulted when he told the Negro gang "to move away" from a tavern at Ogden and Kedzie.

"I was in uniform and some of the lads even knew me," he said.

"I just asked 'em to move on. It was one o'clock in the morning. My request was routine . . . something that you do a lot of times."

* * *

"BUT THE fight started when somebody yelled:

" 'Get that _____'s gun.'

"It seemed like they all jumped me at once. I fought as best I could and tried to keep my gun. But they finally got it away after I was kicked in the face several times and stunned."

Burns, bleeding from his injuries, stumbled to his squad car and summoned help.

Fellow officers soon rounded up 17 toughs. Several were identified as members of the Vice Lords, a West Side teen gang.

* * *

"I STILL can't figure out why they did it," Burns said. "It was such a vicious thing and it started in a flash.

"I'm not bitter at the lads. They've been arrested and a judge in court will decide what to do with them."

Burns expects to get out of Presbyterian — St. Luke's Hospital next week and testify against the youths in North Side Boys Court No. 28.

Eight of the teen toughs are being held in County Jail on assault charges at $5,000 bond.

* * *

JOHN I. STAMOS, chief of the state's attorney's criminal division, said the assault charges shortly may be changed to mayhem.

"We will proceed vigorously in prosecuting this gang that seriously injured a fine police officer," Stamos said.

* * *

BURNS' worry, too, has been about his wife, Ann, 50, who suffered a heart attack last September.

"I got hurt just as my wife was beginning to show progress.

"This trouble of mine is minor compared to hers."

But, two visitors late Thursday solved some of Sgt. Burns' worries.

Police Supt. O. W. Wilson and his top aide, Col. Minor K. Wilson, paid a call.

"You most certainly will have a job with the department as far as we're concerned," said O. W. Wilson.

"You've shown great courage. Our department is quite proud of men such as you."

And, then a big smile finally pushed the creases of worry off Joe Burns' brow.

to tie feathers on the barrels of a Winchester and wave them before the fight. In 1961, when Goat was nineteen, he did that in one fight with the Imperial Chaplains. He was the type that always kept a gun and would never box even though he was big for his age, and he was known for coming up in a crowd and shooting.

"We followed them from the Central Park Theater and we set up an ambush. The only thing that fucked up the deal was the police. They had pulled over the Imperials and we didn't know the police had 'em so we attacked. In those days they didn't have blue and white cars; they had just plain black cars.

"We had the street blocked off and a crossfire set up. The intersection where they came into the block was open, but after they got in there, we had them against a brick wall.

"There was a big street light on the corner, and I was gonna wait until they got into position, run up in front of the street light, wave the shotgun, and that was the time for everybody to start shootin'.

"So I waved the handkerchief, everybody started shootin' and I fired the shotgun. All of a sudden, BANG . . . fuckin' Magnums go to shootin' back.

"The next day we read the paper: two police officers, five members of the Imperial Chaplains shot."

Goat was busted and got two years in the Bridewell, but as he says:

"You know that's a helluva sight when you shootin' a shotgun and nothin' but fire come out and all the scarves are lit up."

Many Lords have been stabbed, shot in the stomach or had their brains knocked out in these gang wars, and Goat's brother Dee Dee was one of many who was killed. To prove how tough he was, Dee Dee often defied death. The first time he got messed up was when he got killed in 1960. Dee Dee was sixteen and Cupid, who was just thirteen, was with him.

"We was playin' basketball around Gregory School — one of those tournaments where everybody puts up a quarter or fifty cents to get in and this is used to buy a trophy or somethin' for the winners. We was comin' from a game and we saw the Cobras. We saw four or five so we didn't pay it no mind. We knew we was gonna fight 'em though.

"There were seven or eight of us, but most of the fellas were a half-block away. When we seen 'em, we didn't know we was gonna fight 'em so soon. We cut out at 'em, but we didn't know that they had some more down the block stashed away.

"First they went to hollerin' 'Mighty Cobras'; then they broke and

ran . . . leadin' us back to the trap. We stopped and was comin' back
when they started hollerin' again, so we broke back at 'em and this time
we just kept goin'.

"We ran right into the trap and they started shootin' on us. They
had about three rifles, one with a scope, and some pistols—bullets was
flyin' all over. Me and Dee Dee and Little Sampson was side by side
runnin'. They shot Dee Dee in the chest and he fell. I thought he had
tripped so I grabbed him and say, come on, man. He got up and we
started ruunin' again. Then he got shot again and he fell. We picked
him up and carried him into a hallway on Thirteenth Street, and he
died in my arms before the police wagon even got there."

When we were at war we had to be creative and Calloway became
war counselor because he was treacherous and knew strategy; he even
read about Alexander the Great and Genghis Khan.

One of the things we did was make a complete map of everybody's
neighborhood. No one had one of ours because we had members in
everybody's group and they didn't have any in ours. We had notebooks
and we would map out the gangways, exit doorways, and different
buildings you had to go through to come out to the streets. Then we
would move in from different directions and meet at a certain place.

We would have a stolen car within a block of wherever we did a
shooting. At that time a car was not reported as stolen until it had been
missing for twenty-four hours, so if you stole it the night of the actual
gangbang, it gave you a day or so. We would park the car in an alley
close to the action and throw the weapons in the trunk when we finished.
The last man through closes the trunk. If everyone couldn't arrive at
the same time, we used cardboard to jam the lock so the lid just closed
and didn't lock. The next day somebody would go by and pick up the car.

Roofs were good places to plan since you can see in all directions,
but sometimes we used basements, schoolyards, anywhere where nobody
could hear. But for an ambush, the best places were gangways and
alleyways because they had outlets. Roofs were no good because you
had to get off the roof, out of the building and down the gangway.

Creative gangbanging was our thing and Calloway used to say, "If
I ever went to the army at a time of war, I'd win somethin' for this
white man's country." One tactic was where we called the police and
told them eighty Lords were going to roll. When the police got there,
there were eighty Lords and they put everybody on the wall, but the
main group was attacking somewhere else.

In an ambush we knew who we were going to get and how we were going to leave the scene of the crime. If there was a group of ten or twelve, we knew who we wanted out of the group and we knew where to find him within the group. If he was a bad joker, he would be up front; if he was a semi-coward, he would be in the middle; and if he was a complete coward, then he wouldn't even be with them: he would be a straggler.

We did a lot of planning for some of the falls because the name of the game is doing it and getting away. Once we spent two months just taking the sweaters off the backs of the Imperial Chaplains and the Cobras. When they united to fight against us and gave a party, we took all the sweaters we had got and sent our own fellas to the party. Goat was in the group that rolled down after they had infiltrated.

"They was jivin' and havin' a motherfuckin' ball and didn't know we had two hundred cats up in that motherfucker with Cobra sweaters. We came to the door a hundred and fifty strong and they say:

"'There the Vice Lords, we gonna get them dudes tonight.'

"They was walkin' around talkin' to our boys and our boys were sayin', 'Yeah, Jack, we gonna jam those motherfuckers, ain't we?'"

Then Goat ran out there with a shotgun and shot all the ceiling out; Calloway threw the juke box down the steps, and the Cobras say:

"All the Cobras step over in this corner."

Nobody moved. The Imperials found out and say:

"You all got our jive on, man."

As Goat says, "We whipped them niggers all night up there and they stopped wearin' their sweaters then."

The success of the club depended on the skills of the club. If there was no skill in the club, you were dead. You needed leadership with creative ideas and you needed leaders who could make a decision, stick with it, and not care how tough it gets; you needed cats that just didn't give a damn.

A guy had status by being good in whatever he did. If he was a gangfighter, he was a good gangfighter. If he wanted to go out south and didn't have carfare, he stole a car and that gave him status. There were guys who could steal any kind of car you wanted. We put Edsel out of business; we stole every one we could find. We used aluminum foil for the wires to jump the starter in Fords and Cadillacs, and screwdrivers for Buicks and Chevys. We also made keys from somebody's daddy's car, then we experimented with other cars of the same make—we had a shoebox full of keys.

You needed cats that wouldn't fight but would be car thieves, hubcap thieves, battery thieves, or just cats with a trade like electricity. But about the only time electricity was used was with the Cobras. They had stolen a car and to stop them from getting away, we connected about ten batteries to the car. They ran out to the car and grabbed the door and a dude stood there for about ten minutes shaking. The paint nearly peeled off the car.

The streets were a jungle and you had to go out and hustle. You didn't have programs and you had to get in the streets to survive. Money came from small rackets like hubcaps, snatching pocketbooks or knocking a dude in the head. Protection required too much bookwork. We wanted something right then and there. A guy in the syndicate was thinking big money, long range, but for us, tomorrow was no big thing. You were stealing, gangbanging and carrying a pistol so something could happen any time. During these years you had to be suspicious of everybody, even your mama, as Toehold says:

"If you was stealin' good, you didn't even tell your girlfriend you was stealin'. She might trick on you or want part of the money and if she didn't get any she would tell the man. You didn't tell nobody your business."

During these gangbanging days the police would bust a dude for no reason. The older fellas remember when police would just walk up on a brother and hit him right dead in his eyes. Some Lords tussled with cops like Gloves Davis because he didn't even identify himself as a policeman. When he approached somebody, he was just another guy on the street. And when he confronted you, you were a bunch of names. If you didn't move fast enough, he'd knock you down. This was when you find out he's a police officer.

Leo Haley was another one. If you were on your way to the corner and Leo Haley is on the corner, automatically you stop, turn around and face the other direction. It didn't matter where you were going or what you were going to do. Once you hear Leo Haley is on the corner, you find somewhere else to go.

There was another cop who was more smooth. He wasn't too quick to just jump on you and beat you up for no reason, but he was still no good. If he was looking for you, on some beef, he would just put his name and phone number on a piece of paper and whip it under your door. When you call him, he says:

"Well, I got you on such and such a beef. You come down and straighten it out. I'll see that you get back home. You'll have time to make your bond and I'll set the date for you to appear."

You go down there and that's it; you're locked up and he tells you to shut your fucking mouth.

Your rights weren't worth anything. A policeman would stop four or five fellas, make a call of policeman in distress, and four more squads would come. They lined up all the fellas against the wall, searched them, took their shirts off and looked for tracks on their arms.

Individuals have certain rights but talking about your rights was foolish. You may be called any and all names and they'll show you where your rights are. You just put your hands up so high your shirttail comes out of your pants.

Jerry remembers that one of his partners, Humpback Ricky, was shot once in the shoulder by the police when he was trying to stick up a bus. He fell and threw up his arms, but the police shot again.

"Pang, pang, pang . . . five more times. I mean once your hands are up in the air it means whatever you done did, it's over. . . you're ready to give up and that should be it."

During one of the riots in the sixties, Calvin was grabbed on his way to the South Side. He didn't have a criminal record and was not doing anything wrong, but when the police grabbed him and three friends:

". . . they started hittin' us up side the head. After this we stood up side the wall, head achin' and shit. They take a blackjack and hit me up side the head—bam! I say, man, do we have to take all this?

"A white policeman, I'll never forget him; he said:

" 'Goddamn, Outlaw (that was a black policeman), you get all the niggers; I just wantta beat me one ass.'

"He had his blackjack and we were in the car handcuffed up to the door. When we got to court, the police lied on us and we told the judge about our constitutional rights. But the best thing for us to do was go ahead and take the time. You try to defend yourself, to speak up for your rights in this world, but if you're black, you're wrong. And two or three more colors, it don't mean shit. You say you gonna demand your rights. You can't demand nothin'!

They would whip the fellas right in the police station too. As the fellas say, its something to have a police officer put a sack on your head and some of them whip you and you can't identify none of them. Or they sit you in a chair and put a telephone book on your head and hit the top of the telephone book with a monkey wrench. You feel the full impact of that monkey wrench on your skull but you won't have no monkey wrench scar.

Any policeman knows how to administer a whipping without the person appearing all beat up when he appears in court. And if you're arrested and seven policeman whip you in the station, you stand a piss poor chance in court telling the judge that seven policemen whipped you and he say which seven and you can't identify them. It's just like all blackies look alike to white folks. When you get a whippin', all policemen look alike.

There were other bad cops and one Lord remembers two of them beating up on a cat when he was handcuffed.

"I saw 'em have one cat handcuffed with his hands behind him in the chair and they just beat him on the stomach with one of them blackjacks . . . the kind they don't use any more, round and a lot of lead. I saw 'em use a rubber hose and when the officer whip you, you be bruised up, but the first thing they say is you resisted arrest and you tried to attack them so they had to do this. But how can a man beat you if he is handcuffed and why does he have bruises now when he had no marks when he got in the squad car? And usually they didn't take the handcuffs off until they take you in the station and kick your ass."

During that time, most of the trouble was from black police. The white police didn't bother us. They didn't have blacks and whites riding in the same car so mostly black police would answer the calls. Most of us felt the white police saw that we were only cutting up and shooting and killing our own people. In a way we did them a favor: that's one less nigger they had to kill.

But the action was both ways because from the fifties to about 1961, the police used to ride the old three-wheel police bikes and gangbangers would whip their ass, take their pistols and run them off. When you had one cop walking the beat, who was he going to catch? All everybody did was circle around and say, "What the hell you want?"

As gangs got guns and the police got organized, the sentences got stiffer. In 1958 you could be seventeen years old and murder another gangbanger and do sixty days in St. Charles and come home. In 1967 you could murder a gangbanger and you would get twenty years before you're eligible for parole.

In 1954 police were rolling on three-wheel motorbikes. You could throw bricks at them all night and never go to jail. In 1969 police ride in squad cars; you throw one brick and get five to ten.

During the early sixties the police gang unit was better than the one they have now. They knew who was who and what was what and where was where and where to go and when. You seldom heard about them coming in your house and jumping on you. They had police that would beat the shit out of you, but they were just officers on duty or detectives in the station. The gang cars took you to the Audy Home, not the police station, and the Audy Home did more good than the jails.

When they started putting guys in jail, more killing and shooting started. When you went to the Audy Home, you stayed until your mama got you out. You washed a few windows or a few walls. But when you went to the County Jail, somebody taught you how to open safes. You got messed up with criminals and at seventeen you became a criminal. So cats say, "What the fuck, we gonna get time so let's be crooks." Even if you try to do something right, the police may run you in, so there is nothing to lose either way you go.

In those days the Vice Lords had no actual rules to follow, but there was a chain of command. You could be a Vice Lord walking down the street and slap a woman down. You were right. But if you did it once and somebody higher than you within the gang said don't do that again and you did it, then you were in trouble. Until that happened, you were free to do what you please. "It was just like the cowhand riding into Dodge City: on Friday night you do what you want; the big bosses come get you later."

Most of the fellas are content just to be members, but there are some who are ambitious and look to get a rep so they can become a chief. In the early years there were about fourteen leaders and they each had lieutenants. There were chiefs and war counselors of the nation, chiefs and war counselors of the branches, and senior, junior and midget groups.

The Nation had an intelligence group, the SCIA, to find out where the enemy was and what he was going to do, pick up rumors and check them out, and if somebody got killed, to find out who did it. Not even the fellas in the club know who all the SCIA members are.

There was also a group known as the Enforcers. These were fifteen to twenty Lords led by Cupid, Wayne, Dino, Pookie, and Charley Booma who kept order in meetings or checked out and dealt with trouble on the street. Whatever rules were made, the Enforcers made sure they were obeyed.

The top leader has to be a little of everything. He's got to be tough and he can't afford to make many wrong decisions. If he does, the group will oust him and somebody else will take over.

The chief is somebody who can be with dope fiends this minute and with the wine heads the next, He can be with the cowards and the guys that are tough. He has to mingle with any type of people.

There have been only two chiefs of the Nation since the Lords began. Pep was the chief until 1964 and Alfonso has been chief since then.

Pep was a good leader because he was smart, tough and violent. He could whip just about everybody in the club and would fight quick, but you have to get along with people because you can't whip a whole gang, and everybody liked him for his wit.

In 1964, when he was twenty-one, Pep began spending more time with his family. But you can't stay at home and expect to run the fellas in the street. A lot of people just like to be around the chief and make sure he's all right, and a cat looks big when he can be with the chief, so the fellas just wanted another chief and one night in the pool room decided on Alfonso Alford. They told Pep and he said that was mellow, and even though Al refused several times, eventually he accepted.

Alfonso had come to Chicago from another city in 1962 and right away everybody liked him. Not any one man could move into the leadership, but Al was cut into the Lords in the proper way. He can get along with anybody, but if you're wrong, he'll let you know and split your head. He's the type the ghetto respects and understands. Even when Peppilow was running the set, there was a crowd of people who just loved Al and stood with him at all times. When Al took over the Lords as chief he was twenty-nine, older than most but one of the fellas in every way. Cupid became one of his top lieutenants.

"We used to go places with him where we'd never been — taverns, shows, drive-ins — and sometimes we'd take five or six carloads and go out to the beach or the forest on a picnic, and usually he'd be spending his own money. I learned how to take care of business from him.

"Al and Goat fixed it up for us to go to Palos Park and stay three days and this gassed us because we never did nothin' like this unsupervised. We went on trips before with the YMCA, but the girls would go one weekend and the boys the next. You can't have no fun with a bunch of boys. You want to be rappin' to girls. You be with the fellas every day.

"Wasn't no one lookin' over us tellin' us you can't do that and you can't do this. You can't go over there but you can go over here. We could do what we wanted to do. If you wanted, you and your lady could sleep together.

"Everybody started gettin' jobs, started keepin' money and cleanin' up the neighborhood. If we had more people like Al, there wouldn't be no violence; if more people thought the way he do, there wouldn't be these problems. He's the type of guy you can bring your problem to and when you leave, one way or the other, somethin' is bein' done about it. And he's not the type of guy that asked anybody for nothin'. But he don't have to ask anyway 'cause all the fellas want to do somethin' for him. The man is just loved—that's all there is to it.''

Monk

Calloway

Sam

Cupid

Pep

Al

Nooney

Billy

Dino

Goat

Before

After   Sixteenth Street

Before

After

After

Al   W. Clement Stone

Homan House of Lords

Street Mural by Don McIlvaine

Street Mural By Don McIlvaine

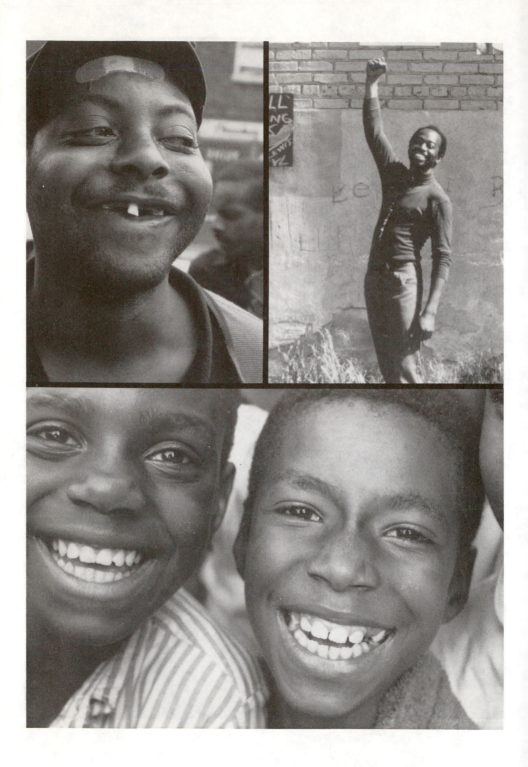

Mayor Richard J. Daley

April 5, 1968

Coming Up

In the sixties the younger fellas made the streets rougher than the older teenagers did. The younger cats — eleven, twelve, thirteen years old — were trying to build a name, and the older ones had families or had to work. The younger ones were trying to be what they had been, and you cannot ignore a dude that can go out and get fifteen or twenty cats together, whether he's good or bad. You got to get him and talk to him to find out what his thing is.

There have been times when the older guys were even fighting the younger ones. The thing was to become as bad as the guy ahead of you. The same as the Old West: whoever killed the fastest draw in the West became the fastest draw and you practiced all your life until you became that fast.

When Goat was young, he had a plan to become a chief. He knew that chiefs are stronger and tougher than the members and they had all the women, and he knew that he must be creative and bold. To prove himself, he decided to create his own war.

"We were young cats and did what we wanted to do and didn't give a fuck what the older dudes wanted to do. But they were tough and to get up with these cats, you got to be as tough as they is. The only way to outdo 'em is to be just as cold-blooded and vicious."

The first thing Goat did was to run down the alley and throw down all the garbage cans. Then he got a group of fellas and broke all the windows in the neighborhood and the people were saying, "We got to lock up those punks."

But the big boys didn't dig the garbage cans or the windows so he had to think of something else. For the next four or five months, he attacked each corner, each group, each playground, each neighborhood around the Lords area. He had established a name but he needed a reputation so the chiefs would recognize him.

One of the fellas in the group had an idea.

"All we got to do, man, if you want to move these guys is take a broad and shoot her, man. We shoot her and then we get her friends and shoot them and we call that initiation."

Goat liked the idea and decided to try it.

"I got a broad, we shot her in the arm, and all the police in the world come and the whole neighborhood says who are these cats that shot the girl. So we was the bad dudes and everybody walked around with their chest stuck out: 'We shot a broad in the arm yesterday; you guys ain't done nothin like this.'

"So the president says, 'You gotta stop shootin' folks; when you shoot people you bring in the police.' And we say, Well, dig, we gonna shoot a whole lotta people. We ain't even started shootin'.

"So they say, 'Why you doin' this, man? What's the beef?'

"We told them we want to be the war counselors and to make us the war counselors or we're gonna kill everybody we see. They say we better make these fools the war counselors and get somethin' on their minds 'cause they're sick. So they made us war counselors, which was a horrible thing to do because we made war on every club that was around."

CHICAGO DAILY NEWS, July 11, 1961
Boy, 16, ACCUSED
IN GIRL'S SHOOTING

A 16-year old boy with a record since he was 12 for strongarm robbery was identified Tuesday as the youth who shot and wounded a 5-year-old girl with a homemade zip gun.

The boy, _____, of S. Karlov, apparently was trying to qualify for membership on a teen gang, police said.

He was identified by the victim's grandmother, Mrs. Hilda B. Morris.

_____, 14, of W. 14th St. was seized also.

The victim, Patricia Harris, 3604 W. 15th St. was shot in the right hip as she played with other tots on a sidewalk Monday. Physicians said the wound was superficial.

Travis Pumphrey, an off-duty Fillmore district policeman, seized the two youths.

Pumphrey said he learned from other youngsters in the area that shooting a woman or a girl was part of the initiation for a splinter gang of the notorious Vice Lords.

The new gang calls itself the "Mafia."

"There's a struggle for leadership going on," Pumphrey said, "These kids will do anything to show the others what big men they are."

Police said three youths approached the girl and one of them fired without warning. After a foot chase lasting 20 minutes, Pumphrey caught two of them.

For many of the young fellas in the neighborhood, the Vice Lords was the only thing happening. When Elzy moved to Lawndale from another neighborhood, the first thing he heard about was Vice Lords. The Lords were just starting and a lot of people were getting jumped on. His mother got him assigned to a program in the Morrissey Center, but instead of going, Elzy went to a place where the fellas met, called the Hole in the Wall. He was about eight or nine years old.

"I had a little dough and the first thing I started doin' around there was rippin' off bullets for the older dudes. We would go to Sears and steal bullets and guns. We was goin' through that roguin' bag when you rip off somethin' as a status symbol.

"Then my mind developed to where I say, damn, I been rippin' off long enough; now I want to do somethin'. I want to get out there and humbug some. At that time we were Royal Knights and the old Vice Lords thought that we couldn't relate to them so we kicked off our own thing."

The Vice Lords were the first to get pee wees, then the Cobras decided to get some. There were three divisions: pee wees (midgets), juniors, and seniors. The pee wees were nine to thirteen and included L'il Fool, Caveman, and Big Otis. They used to rip off pop trucks, cookie trucks, and bread trucks and fight with groups like the Black Hawks, the Vultures, and the Jets, but every time the big fellas started to roll, they were told to stay back.

Some people say that older guys had the young ones make hits for them because the younger ones would just go through juvenile court if they were caught, but there was nothing for the older guy to gain in telling a younger cat to do this. He could get just as much time and couldn't make any money. But in 1961 and 1962 when the Lords would get in a humbug, young cats coming up were watching and learning from everything that went on.

People in the community would crowd up to see what was going on, and one day at the corner of Fifteenth and Lawndale, Ting was one of the young cats who came out to watch.

"Me and a coupla more young dudes were sittin' down there on the curb lookin' at 'em humbug, and the lead was just steady poppin' over our head. Later on the Vice Lords started comin' around, and they got respect because they had a game about themselves.

"What they believed in they were wiling to die for, and if another cat went through a hood and got jumped on, the Vice Lords rolled. He didn't even have to be a Lord, just live in the community.

"Young kids knew 'em by name, and the people gave the Vice Lords respect because they knew they didn't mess around, and this was during the gangbang era. The only way they gave some kind of fear is if you lived in the Vice Lords territory and you were a Cobra.''

The YMCA had a street work program but the workers had no control. They had workers that were assigned to the groups if we accepted them, but we used to fire one every two weeks. They took us swimming and camping, but all they really did was hang around. The only way we let them stay was for the Y to put some fellas on the payroll as consultants and field assistants. They just gave us money to let a worker stay and he was supposed to find out the problems and take it back to the Y, and they were supposed to find a way to deal with them. But the worker knew only what you wanted him to know and if he found out something that you didn't want him to know, he'd better not tell.

We didn't need a social worker and we didn't ask for one. The fellas felt that having one was like going to church on Sunday. Nobody went to church and nobody needed a preacher.

Wayne was eleven in 1959 and 15 in 1963, and during that time his heroes were Pep, Mad Dog (killed in a gangbang), and Son. He wanted to be like them because you could walk up to them and just start a fight. In 1964, when some of the older fellas started talking about changes, Wayne thought it was something that would never come about. But there were guys Wayne respected from the street like Bobby Gore who were rapping that new thing.

"Bobby used to talk to me all the time. I wouldn't listen to him because I thought he just be jokin' around. During that time, people didn't know Vice Lords as young businessmen like today; they just pictured 'em as old-fashioned gangbangers.''

By 1968 the young cats coming up saw something different.

"I feel less violence now. Ain't too much happenin' and ain't nobody rollin'. This is the only way I can see a community build up. It's the latest thing—no violence. And I can dig it. I sure can dig it.''

Elzy had felt different when he was young.

"Look, they was doin' what they was supposed to be doin'. I'm a rebel. I didn't dig traditions 'cause I was educated traditionally in the jive ass Catholic school and all that bullshit. But I had this vision that this kind of thing wasn't right.''

Cupid felt he had no choice when he was young. There was no place to go, and you had to sign papers to join some of the recreation clubs.

It was years before his parents knew he was in a gang.

I used to come home whipped up and what not, and I told them a gang jumped on me 'cause I wouldn't join, but I was already in a gang, and I probably started the fight. They finally got hip to me and went to whippin' me, but it didn't do no good. I kept on doin' it.

"I used to go to Gregory School and I lived about a block away. I wouldn't go and just ditched; I'd hang with some of the big fellas across the street from the school in the basement of a building. My teacher kept seein' me out there but never in school so she called my mother up one day and it just so happened I was out there struttin' with my cape on. When I got ready to go home, I'd take the cape to one of my friend's house and leave it 'til the next day.

"The teacher showed my mother where I was, and my mother told her I was supposed to be in school. That evening when it was time for me to come home from school, she didn't say nothin'. I ate and went out to play and got my cape again and went to clownin'. About that time, my father got home from work and that's what she was waitin' for. She told him and when I came home that night about ten, I got ready for bed and cut the light out. The next thing I know the light was on, the cover was snatched, and I was gettin' whipped.

"That didn't do any good. I just kept on doin' the same thing. It was just the type of life I liked at that time. School didn't interest me and most of the time when I did go, me and the teacher would get into it. Once a teacher hit me with a ruler so I went back and as he was sittin' at the desk, I hit him across the head with a chair."

The feeling of most of the young fellas was that you don't have to go to school to learn what you need to know; all you have to do is get out here in the streets.

Some would quit school ("We got to messin' around with them broads so much they made us quit school and then didn't do nothin'") and those that didn't quit were thrown out. At lunchroom one day, a group were talking about a teacher and they called him O.B. Skull. They made Ting laugh so hard he went over and told O.B. that he ought to cut them cats because they were talking about his head. O.B. took Ting to the assistant principal and had him suspended for a month. When he got back to school and saw O.B., Ting shouted down the corridor: "I'm gonna fuck you up, O.B."

Schools don't understand most of the young cats, so when a dude gets in high school, he feels like Jerry that "this thing is really terrible, man, when you try for yourself and nobody else can help you. They'll tell you they'll help you, and they'll help some but only to an extent. When they see you got a mind for yourself and you're progressin', that help begins to drop. And once it begins to drop, you say, well, I tried to help myself and what did they do? As help slacked, I couldn't take it alone—it was too much of a burden, man.

"So you just say, fuck it, I'm goin' back to my street life—bustin' peoples in the head and takin' their paycheck every Friday. It's really no good but that's your only alternative."

When you turn sixteen, you consider yourself a man, and around Lawndale, boys are trained to be men when they are young. But the white person looks at you and says this man's thing stays too hard all the time. If schools don't respect them as men, the young cats get the feeling that Elzy has, "that on the street we don't have to conform to any bullshit traditions that have been laid down. If you want to lay out on Sixteenth, it's good. We're not gonna go home because that's civilized authority—we can't cut that. So we gonna stay up here, we gonna bop it down, smoke it down, and oil it down, and in a sense, this is revolution."

1967

A Change Is Gonna Come

One evening in July, 1964, Al, Bobby, Cal, Pep, and J.W. were sitting around in the sixteen hundred block of Lawndale, drinking wine and throwing bottles into the empty yard — or out in the damn street; it didn't make us no difference.'' One of the younger fellas said he wanted to make a fall with about fifty others. The chiefs asked him why and who he wanted to fall on and had anyone misused him. He said that the older Lords now in their twenties had made a name and they wanted to keep it alive.

They sat up all night and the chiefs told the younger dudes how they had seen people begging not to be hit any more with a baseball bat or chain, how guys got cut up, how the people and police would hate their guts, and how one of them might get killed. Finally one of the younger fellas said:

''Well, we have to do somethin'. We can't get jobs, we're too old to go back to school, and we're too big to play games. What else is there to do?''

The fellas looked around and saw how many had been killed, hurt, or sent to jail and decided they didn't want the younger fellas coming up to go through the things they did and get bruises and scars and wounds from gangfighting. Instead of all this fighting, Al decided that they should do something constructive like try to open some businesses.

The fellas talked about it, but it didn't sound right. We were getting our kicks from just drinking and fighting so we said:

''Man, we can't do that. You know these honkies ain't gonna give us nothin'.''

But Al insisted, ''All we gotta do is try.''

So the fellas started thinking and reasoning with each other to stop this gang war and get some fat on the head. Eventually by dealing with the younger brothers, we found out what fools we had been.

103

In 1969 Bobby was thirty-two and, looking back, he thought, "Rather than get pats on the back for what we're doing now, we need to be kicked in the ass 'cause we should have been doing this ten years ago. And my old man needs to be kicked in his ass 'cause he ain't told me nothin'. His old man needs to be kicked in his ass and you can take it all the way back. You just can't sit there in silence and let this kinda thing go on and let your son grow up to be misused. You gotta see that your kids have a better chance. To hell with us. Our lives are wasted."

The most common feeling on the West Side of Chicago has been one deeply felt by most black people: the feeling of hopelessness. You can work each week, five days a week, and when Friday comes, when that eagle flies, you have to put fifteen dollars on this, twenty on that, thirty on something else and you don't have anything left. You work, work, work, come home and sleep and on Saturday all you can do is stand on the corner or walk around the street because you don't have any money. So you look at yourself and say I ain't workin' for nothin' and you snatch somebody on the collar and take his money. If you ain't got it, you got to go out and get it 'cuz you got to have it.

In 1964 the Lords vowed to see that our community and children get a chance, and three years later, as spokesman for the Nation, Bobby said:

We could not turn our backs on them. We were and are the last resort for many, and if we didn't listen, who would?

"Buckney[1] and them can knock me off tomorrow, or whoever the hell it is . . . a jealous-hearted dude, like they got King, like they're after Jackson.[2] Well, this is these cats that's sick in the mind and the reason they're sick in the mind is because whoever did the job on 'em did a damn good job, and it's time for us to try and reverse this shit.

"These cats see that we ain't got but one humbug and that's to get our asses out of the sand and stand up like men. We been resolved to the thing that we ain't nobody, ain't gonna never be shit. But like the Reverend say: I am somebody!

"I might be in the penitentiary, but I'm somebody. I might be the worse dude in the world; I might be a stickup man, but I'm somebody.

As black people, we gotta start worryin' about what's happening, where our real humbug is and the way to humbug with it."

The Lords had to try to change the conditions that make a cat get a gun and hold up a store, that make him drink scrap iron to forget about the lousy conditions he lives in, that lead a dude to hustle dope and to leave the family he wants to support but cannot.

[1] Captain Edward Buckney, Gang Intelligence Unit, Chicago Police Department.
[2] The Reverend Jesse Jackson, former director of Operation Breadbasket.

We wanted to build up the community so we started trying to give the people a new outlook. Most people still considered us a gang, but we were trying to get over to them that we were becoming an organization to help our brothers and sisters and that we were no longer out for killing and jive.

If somebody don't straighten this shit out, then our kids are going to be misused. Goat found this out in the penitentiary and this was his reason for going along with the others.

"I was a fucking god; I was idoled by cats I had never met. I be walkin' down the fuckin' gallery and the guy say, Mr. Goat this, Mr. Goat that. Guys would ask if I was goin' back to the fellas when I got out and 'Can I look you up when I get out?' or 'Where do I go from here?'

"I didn't know where the hell to tell 'em to go 'cause I wasn't goin' back to gangbanging. There was no future in it and you went only two ways: pen the rest of your life or death. It took about nine times of goin' to jail before I found out that ain't where it's at. I got in a place with the guys I used to idol and they weren't goin' any place and they couldn't answer me.

"I saw myself forty years from now in their fuckin' shoes and this is when I found out. See, that's when I started to say, wait a minute. . . let me stop for a minute and slow down.

"Then I went to thinkin'. What happened to gangs before my gang? I found out they were minus because either they was still doin' life in the pen or were paralyzed or their mothers were takin' them flowers on Memorial Day. So I say, where do I go not to get in this category, and there was only one other way to go."

For others, there may be some form of violence, age or a personal experience that scares them into changing. For Jerry, there was a robbery. He and two others were together and they needed some money.

We had about forty or fifty cents apiece, but George says this ain't enough. We were sittin' on the porch and we had a crowbar so we say let's go get some more. So this man walked up and say, 'Hey fellas, you wantta get a drink?' and he pulled out a little bankroll and everybody looked at each other like, hey, we get this cat.

"I just couldn't stand hittin' a person with a crowbar so I stood in the way of George and tried to grab him so he don't hit him in the head. Before I know anything, blood was shootin' outta his head. I turned and grabbed my face. They say, 'Come on, man, and get the money,' but I say I don't want none. I say that's my last robbery. I don't want any.

Jerry feels the reason the robbery happened like that is because George had been through the years when blood was no big thing. It was just something somebody could shed, and if they didn't die they could recover.

Another Lord was standing by a friend, also a Lord, when he was killed on the corner of Sixteenth and Lawndale.

"We got a place we call the Iron Curtain where we drink and we was back there drinkin'. Somebody came and told me:

"'Say, man, you betta come on the corner 'cause I think there's somethin' wrong. They over there arguin' and clownin' and pushin' on each other.'

"I'm not thinkin' 'cause this is the type of life every weekend—somebody gettin' high, and they get arguin' and fistfightin'—you wouldn't be human if you didn't do that in the life we live. So when I'm drinkin' I hear gunshots, and me and about eight others break out and across, tryin' to find out what's goin' on.

"By the time we get there I dig him staggerin' and stumblin' and blood just gushin' out of his head like a fountain. He was just spinnin' around and fallin' and I tried to catch him but I was drunk. We both fell and his brains and stuff was on my shirt and my arm.

"I've seen a lotta dudes but never like that. I never been that close up on it 'cause when I caught him and his brains and stuff fell on me, that shook me up. I've seen 'em die before in wars and gang fights; I've seen some of my fellas die and other fellas too but not like that."

Like Wayne says, "You don't have to look for trouble on Sixteenth. It comes to you."

But we have come a long way from the time when a Lord couldn't walk down Sixteenth Street without a paddy wagon stopping him, when the businesses closed at six for fear of guys snatching pocketbooks and when the only ladies up and down the street were vice Ladies.

In the three years from 1964 to 1967 we stopped gang wars and started to build a new kind of Vice Lord Nation—Vice Lords even began living in K-Town. Between 1967 and 1969 we opened several businesses and community programs. The police never thought they would see the day when we'd put our minds to do something like that. They always considered us gangbangers. Not even the younger fellas thought we could change.

The gangbanging stopped for a number of reasons. The chiefs saw that the younger cats were coming up like they had and that this was a dead end, and some guys cut the gang loose because they got shot up or locked up. Another reason was that people started to think about civil rights.

The militants came in and say why be a gangbanger and kill each other when you can kill the honky, and we began to see that the enemy was not black. Elzy, who was about twenty and had been on the streets for eight years as a Royal Knight and junior Vice Lord, felt that "we were scared of the honkies, but this awareness thing has kicked all that bullshit aside and made you think of what you really are."

In 1969, Toehold saw that "whitey have tricked us to fight among ourselves. He have turned our own wives against us, turned some of the fellas own mothers against 'em. It's whitey's thing. Two years ago I wouldn't have thought like this, but I have made meetings and now I say whitey is the cause of blacks fighting blacks."

When the riots started in Watts in 1965, most people felt kind of good and proud because somebody could do something like that. The Lords saw films and Pep was one who felt that Watts inspired many people in Chicago.

"Even though a lot of them got killed or hurt, all the black people say this enlightened the younger generation of blacks. They say, 'Damn right,' and then it started spreadin'. Everywhere you go, black people were sayin', 'You damn right.' Even some of the police would come up and say, "You must want another Watts, nigger."'"

This was imbedded so deep in the hearts of black people that the next year there was bound to be something in the big city ghettos—like Detroit, Cleveland and Chicago.

We felt the pressure of the white man constantly in Lawndale, and in a sense, suburban Mississippi was right across the street. We felt the same pressure that the people in Mississippi have been feeling, only our pressure was more modern. Down South they have white sheets on, but in Lawndale they have blue sheets. Instead of coming into our house at night lynching us, they catch us on the corner, give us time, harass us, take us off and beat us. Or they take things from us and try to tell us what not to wear on our heads, what not to wear on our bodies. We might have a sweater with the club name and the police would tear it off, or if we had a scarf on, they wanted to tear that off.

At night we couldn't go across Cicero Avenue into the village of Cicero. We could work there, we could clean their houses and sweep their streets; but when it got dark we had to leave. We couldn't go to their nice schools and we couldn't go to the nice restaurants in the wee hours of the night.

That was suburban Mississippi: Cicero, Illinois. They talked about the same things down South that they talked about here.

Civil rights showed us that if our fathers had stood up at the time, we wouldn't have to go through the things that we are going through now to make a better life. We wouldn't have to die.

But as black people, we didn't know we had these rights. We didn't know we could sit in the front of the bus. We didn't know that a dude couldn't refuse us because we were human beings. The only thing we knew is what our forefathers told us: Don't upset the white man.

We got tired of this and said we're going to put up a scuffle even though we may lose. We didn't need SNCC and CORE and SCLC to kick off a riot in 1966. Gangbangers were involved because young dudes just didn't have any other way to go. This was just a helluva way to let go of the frustrations and depression.

The civil rights organizations that came to Chicago were not working with the hard-core people anyway. They were supposed to have been for the grass root but the middle class was running them. They didn't know the people. The people who wouldn't mind being in a riot were never touched. They were still out there standing on the corners, laying in the alleys, and in the summertime sleeping in the park at night.

The 1966 riot in Chicago started around Memorial Day when some white dude jumped on a black dude with a baseball bat and killed him. He was cut loose and they said the black dude was down there inciting a riot. Actually he was getting off work and waiting for the bus when three or four white boys came up with the baseball bat and got to beating him. He didn't have a chance of living because his brain was beat to a pulp.

This riot was not well organized and there was just a lot of looting and breaking. Yancey ran into a store, took off his overcoat and put on a new one, got a new hat, new undershirt, pants, socks, shoes and came out clean. He even took another wardrobe to wear later on during the week.

During the riot the sister of a Vice Lord was killed in the crossfire of a gun battle with the police. She was pregnant and the baby died in her. At her funeral in the Stone Temple Church, the Lords again decided to try and start something so the next time, the police would think twice before they start shooting.

This was when SCLC came in. Martin Luther King came on the West Side and had an apartment on Hamlin and Sixteenth about two blocks from the Lords pool room. In his place King was beautiful, but we weren't going to march and have people throw stones without throwing some back.

CHICAGO DAILY NEWS
Tuesday, January 25, 1966

DR. KING'S NEW ADDRESS JUST OFF
'BLOODY 16TH ST.'

BY EDMUND J. ROONEY

The truck driver stopped to answer the question after making a delivery across the street from the old beat-up building into which the Rev. Martin Luther King will move Wednesday.

"What's this neighborhood like?" asked the visitor.

"Rough, man. Really rough. We call it ol' bloody 16th St. and that's sure what it is.

"Junkies, stick-up men, muggers. They're around day and night. And they're mean. You gotta be tough, too, or they'll walk all over you trying to get your money."

It was midafternoon in North Lawndale. And 16th St. teemed with people.

In 1857, immigrant Dutch and German settlers walked peacefully across the undeveloped prairie that was then part of Cicero Twp., land that was later annexed as a Chicago residential section.

Today, more than 130,000 Negros — mostly impoverished — are crammed into the blocks near King's cheap third-floor walkup flat at 1550 S. Hamlin.

It is from these four rooms that Nobel Peace Prize winner King expects to direct most of his upcoming massive assault on the city's slums and discrimination.

King earlier this month told reporters that he personally wanted to live in one of Chicago's most depressed slum areas for several reasons.

"I don't want to be a missionary in Chicago but an actual resident in a slum section so that we can deal firsthand with the problems. We want to be in a section that typifies all the problems that we're seeking to solve in Chicago."

King and his aides will find the area from Kedzie to Pulaski a string of rundown taverns, resale stores, storefront churches, pool halls and slum buildings.

Some North Lawndale residents term it Slumdale. The average family's yearly income here is estimated at 3,200.

King, too, can expect to find the notorious Vice Lords, a Negro teen-age gang estimated to have 1,000 to 3,000 members who make this urban badland their home.

And there already have been rumbles among the Vice Lords to "do something" about King's arrival.

However, many of King's new neighbors say he'll be most welcome.

"He should have been here a long time ago," said one man at the bar in Barbara's Place, 3808 W. 16th St.

The tall man running the Playboy Stick Hall, 3736 W. 16th, was happy, too.

"King's coming up here will spruce up the neighborhood," he said. "The landlords will be getting busier, too. And you can be sure the cops will keep the corner at Hamlin clean all the time."

But probably the happiest of all was the 8-year old schoolboy who lives in the same building as King.

"Good," he said. "Now maybe we'll get some heat in our rooms."

Cupid used to say, "I don't believe in those nonviolent marches where those honkies be throwin' at me and I can't throw back. I can't sing no brick off my motherfuckin' head. I just can't overcome. If a motherfucker hit you, knock that motherfucker down."

King invited the Lords, Blackstone Rangers, and Disciples to a rally at Soldiers Field, but during the rally one of King's people made the statement that they don't need gangbangers. Cupid was in a group that heard the remark.

"Wasn't nobody eavesdropping, or nothin' . . . just some people standin' around. We heard one of Kings men say he didn't feel that he needed all these gangfighters because they weren't goin' to do nothin' but disrupt the rally. Another of King's men, Reverend Sampson, told him it wasn't his place to decide on who you needed and how to get things done.

"I brought it back to Pep and said if the dude feel this way and he's supposed to be King's number one man, then we don't know how King feels and I believe we're frontin' ourselves off. Pep say there wasn't no reason for us to stay there so we rapped with the other groups and when we gave our signal, all the Lords, Stones, and D's stood up and just split. When we left, the place was half empty and that left the King naked.

Later King sent somebody down to set up a meeting in his apartment so Pep, Bobby, and a couple others went over to find out what was happening. King said he didn't know who made the statement but he did need us. He said that he would need the troops, and we knew he needed the troops.

During the summer of 1966 everybody wanted to get in touch with the Lords. The Deacons of Defense, RAM, ACT, and all these different organizations came to the West Side. We would sit and talk to these people, and then some of the older Lords looked at each other and realized that everybody was coming to the Lords.

At this time we were hanging at the pool room at 3655 West Sixteenth Street. Only the fellas over eighteen could go in; the younger Lords had to hang outside so Alfonso and Robert Stanley bought the pool room with money they had hustled and put up a sign that said: "Lawndale Pool Room, CVL—where all the fellows meet." We had a public telephone, a couch in the back and pictures on the wall to show the fellas what was going on. We began traveling again and getting in parades, like the Bud Billiken parade, and we started meeting people and helping people more than we had.

The winter of 1967 brought the Big Snow and with that came looting that lasted for a couple days and nights. The snow buried cars and bus drivers slept in the buses. Police cars tried to make it through but there wasn't anything moving. Finally they had to use helicopters to get in. The young fellas were running around like it was a party, and Ting was with them.

"I can't remember nothin' durin' the big snow 'cause I was gettin' just as high as I want to be. We got all the food and cigarettes and things we needed, then we came back and started stealin' beer, pop, cake, and gave a mistletoe party. We'd get to hawkin' and go over to this other cat's crib, man, and smoke a fourth or half a pound and we would get it on. "Every Jew that owned a store from Cicero damn near all the way back to Western got ripped off.''

Everybody thought the city would blow again in the summer of 1967. This was when we met George Simms, the black commander of the Fillmore Police District; George Collins, the black alderman of the Twenty-Fourth Ward,[3] and David Dawley, in Chicago for the summer to do research on the attitudes of youth toward federally funded summer programs.

Commander Simms was a fair-minded guy, but if you were wrong, he said the only thing that would beat you to the station would be the headlights on the wagon.

Alderman Collins did what he could from his office and opened doors to people who could go a step further than he could, but his hands were tied by the Democratic machine.

Dave was working for the TransCentury Corporation and they had a contract to do research in eleven cities for the President's Council on Youth Opportunity. We met one night at a West Side rally where he was the only white. Chuck Curry, a black street worker, told us that Dave wanted to make contact with the Lords. Pep and Bobby spoke with Dave and made arrangements to meet again at the pool room. During that meeting, Al and Bobby talked with Dave, and we agreed to work together during the summer.

There was no guarantee that the research would change federal programs, but there was a good possibility that the report would get to the people who had the power to make some changes if they wanted to. Since nobody had bothered to ask these questions before, the Lords cooperated.

÷ George Collins later became a United States Congressman. He was killed in an airplane crash in December 1972.

Dave gave Bobby a job as an interviewer, used several Lords as consultants, and one day even rented the pool room to talk with a large group of Lords. He slept at the local YMCA but lived on the street. By the end of summer, we respected each other and we were friends.

One of the new attempts to get some help was started during the summer when Commander Simms and Alderman Collins helped CVL form Operation Bootstrap, a West Side coalition of street groups and industry. The street groups were the Lords, Egyptian Cobras, and Roman Saints, and the business members included Sears Roebuck, which had national headquarters on the West Side, Ryerson Steel, Illinois Bell Telephone, Western Electric, and many others.

We poured our hearts out to these businessmen and they decided to give us a chance to prove our sincerity. They had offices on the West Side and stood to lose millions if more riots broke out, so they agreed to cooperate. In return for cooperation, we promised there would not be a single member of our clubs who would participate in burning or looting of stores. We also promised to help stop these actions. As a result we broke up a number of undercover meetings and in 1967 we had a cool summer.

One of the actions we stopped was when the Panthers were talking about tearing up everything on the West Side. We didn't see eye to eye because we didn't see what we could gain by tearing it up. But we could see what we could gain by not tearing it up or letting anyone else tear it up. The way we looked at it, if we tore up and burned up everything, we wouldn't have any place to go in the winter.

The Panthers wanted the Lords, Cobras, Saints, ACT, and everyone to just start tearing up and meet at a certain place. We took troops and told them that they weren't coming down to tear up anything and if they did come down, they would have to leave some of us laying in the street.

They didn't come.

Another problem developed when a white rookie cop from the Fillmore District shot a sixteen-year-old black youth. Commander Simms called in the street leaders and explained what facts he had and asked for our help in stopping rumors.

We stayed up all night going from corner to corner, talking to cats who thought we should do something, and we managed to keep the lid on.

Sometimes, though, we got into trouble even when we were trying to keep down trouble. This happened to Bobby once in 1967 after Cupid's father was killed when some people tried to rob him. All the young cats wanted to go down through the neighborhood where these cats came from, and Bobby was out there to keep everything under control.

"I was down on the end to send back any fellas, and other chiefs were out there with the cats to keep them from coming down. When I went back, the chief had busted a couple of young cats with a sawed-off shotgun and a couple of pistols. I told him my sister stays right down the street and I would take the shotgun down there.

"I was going through the alley and gangways and a police car rolled up. I knew they were gonna arrest me because I did have the shotgun, but I tried to explain what was going on and that we had called the Alderman and some other people to make them aware that we were out here trying to break up some trouble. Without some communication, we know the police might roll down on us, and once they take us off the street, there's no telling what these young cats might do.

"I put the shotgun down on the ground, and once they snatched that off the ground and put the handcuffs on me, they went to searchin' me and pattin' me. They were so excited and waiting for me to make some old phony move that they pat all over the damn pistol.

"There were two white policemen and a Negro sergeant and one of the white ones accused me of being on the corner shooting at people. I showed him where the gun had not been fired, but all he talked about was killing me from the time they busted me 'til we went in the court. I believe they would have killed me if it hadn't been for the Negro sergeant.

When I got out of the car, I kind of jumped a little and the pistol fell to the ground right out in front of the police station and they didn't notice. They were so busy pushin' me and shovin' me and sayin' who the hell do you think you are that they missed the gun. It might still be out there.

"I ain't sayin' all these cats are bad because we got some out here that I actually believe in. We have worked with Commanders McCann[3] and Simms and we have learned to deal with these men. We have had disagreements and when we're wrong they don't bite their tongue to tell us. We deal with each other as men and we chew each other out. When we come out we know what each other is going to do."

Throughout the summer of 1967, we held meetings at Western Electric and Sears Roebuck. Bootstrap formed a committee for education, a committee for recreation and a committee for law, order, and justice.

[4] Commander William McCann, Marquette District, Chicago Police Department.

Each of these committees had subcommittees and before we knew what was happening, we were back into the same old bag.

The businessmen had agreed to cooperate but they were reluctant to come out and say what they actually felt. In the first meeting of Bootstrap we talked about how West Side business could help the youth groups develop programs. In the second meeting there were social agencies like the YMCA and Youth Action, the street work program.

At the end of the summer, Bootstrap was still talking. Dave went back to Washington to finish the TransCentury report, but he came back on his own in November to develop programs.

This is what he wrote to friends in Washington:

> There's an untold story in Chicago that ghetto youth are organized and looking for help — ''a hand up, not a hand out.'' This phenomenon, new for gangs and unfamiliar to the community, raises these questions: Can we join with organizations created by ghetto conditions to confront problems of poverty? Is the government willing to work with youth with police records? Is big business prepared to invest in community renewal through direct collaboration with an element whose history is brutal but whose present commitment is honest?''
>
> The constructive mood of the Vice Lords and the potential for effective action has been for me the most unexpected and exciting observation of the summer. I have the strong feeling that Lawndale is a frontier for solutions to urban disorder.
>
> We've talked of the need to reach ''hard core'' unemployed youth so why not invest in those that have been ambitious enough to organize and daring enough to attempt change.
>
> Unlike New York, Washington and other cities, there are gangs in Chicago with members from crib to thirty, and unlike Honduras where as Peace Corps volunteers we had to overcome the resistance to work collectively, they have leaders with control and popular support.
>
> Through the Vice Lords, we have an opportunity to develop the most exciting social action project in America — the possibility of organizing a large section of one of the major cities in the United States and of building a new model of social and economic development.
>
> The Vice Lords have demonstrated good faith by meeting throughout the summer with police, businessmen and bureaucrats. While other cities have had riots, the Vice Lords, Roman Saints and Cobras have assisted the city-wide campaign to ''keep a cool summer.'' But without money, without a vote of confidence, at least a test of intentions, the Vice Lords will remain cut off from society as a hoodlum group.

Alderman Collins had kept his end of the agreement. He had promised to help CVL build an ice cream parlor if the summer was cool. By the fall the Alderman had helped to incorporate CVL as a nonprofit organization and work had begun on an old storefront at the corner of Sixteenth and Lawndale.

Dave saw that Bootstrap was doing nothing and that even though we had legal papers of incorporation, that didn't mean anything on the street; Teen Town was moving slowly so we still didn't have a single program.

During this time we also tried to open an employment office. We were promised that the office would be open in a few weeks, so we told Bootstrap that we would use the pool room until the office was ready.

But the employment office never was opened and in January 1965 the police arrested four Lords in the pool room because they were minors. Three of them were on Bootstrap committees and one had just come from the Urban Training Center. They were not shooting pool but waiting to see if there was a meeting for them to attend The officers came in and even refused the I.D. that one of them showed. We felt this was revenge for a complaint that Dave had signed against Officer Gloves Davis, particularly because Davis had told his friends that he was out to get CVL members because he had a grudge against the club.

He proved this by raiding the pool room and by slapping down a Vice Lady in the street. The Vice Lady told how she was waiting for a cab on the night of January 15, 1968 at 12:30 A.M. when Gloves snatched her in the collar and said, "Bitch, I'll beat your black ass." She complained to the Internal Inspections Division of the Chicago Police Department that Gloves beat her, but they said there was not enough evidence to substantiate the charge.

Bootstrap was not listening the way we thought they should and they did not have the resources we needed, so in December 1967 we sent a proposal to the Rockefeller Foundation. In the proposal, we asked for fifteen thousand dollars for three months to put together programs for the summer of 1968. Time was important, and Dave knew that an officer of the Rockefeller Foundation could approve a grant up to fifteen thousand without a full board of directors meeting, so this is all we asked for—something to get us started as soon as possible.

The TransCentury report, "From the Street," had recommended more involvement of youth and earlier planning of summer programs. We didn't need a report to know that programs had been ineffective in involving the hard core, but we used these recommendations in our proposal.

Dr. Joseph Black at the Rockefeller Foundation got back to us right away and told us we should have more money for more time. Meanwhile he was checking us out with the YMCA, which by then was running Bootstrap.

Bootstrap didn't have any money, but John Root, chairman of

Bootstrap and head of the YMCA, saw a chance to get on the bandwagon and committed Bootstrap to match the Rockefeller grant. Part of the understanding was that CVL would help raise the Bootstrap money.

Bootstrap had seen that we weren't waiting for all those meetings and had gone to the outside since they were so slow. This was going to be embarrassing for Bootstrap since all those companies had been meeting for months and hadn't produced anything. According to one executive at the Rockefeller Foundation, the Foundation knew this and used some muscle to get a matching grant even though they probably would have given us the fifteen thousand anyway. So actually we made Bootstrap do something by going to the foundations ourselves and eliminating the middleman. When they saw that we had written a proposal that the Rockefeller Foundation was going to fund, they got more interested. Sears Roebuck even brought in carpenters, plumbers and electricians for Teen Town.

The Rockefeller Foundation gave us the grant to give us a chance to prove ourselves to society — a gang is not supposed to have enough sense to do nothin' but fight and do time. But we were tired of doing time and the grant was a chance to develop new goals and programs to meet these goals. We had six months to develop a plan for CVL.

The YMCA became fiscal agent for the Rockefeller grant because CVL did not have federal tax exemption. We applied in early 1968, but the Internal Revenue Service has still never ruled one way or the other. The agreement with the YMCA was that CVL would determine how the money would be spent and the YMCA would just set up procedures to see that the money went where we said it should go. We didn't want any money unless we had control.

In the beginning the YMCA tried to run the whole grant under Bootstrap; they didn't understand that the YMCA and Bootstrap were separate programs. We didn't want any tricks or any strings and we had to tell them in so many words not to fuck with the money and not to make our grant from Rockefeller look like a Bootstrap program. After we got this straight, we worked well with the YMCA. John Root agreed that the YMCA would be fiscal agent for every grant we got after that, and Henry Thomas set up the books.

We kept having problems with Bootstrap but not with the YMCA. We told Bootstrap that we would welcome the help of industry, government or any other organization from the bottom of our hearts but that all CVL programs must be CVL owned and managed. We are the grass root people; we know who needs help and we can get help to them where others have failed. We said they should not mistake our need for help with our acceptance of their control.

We got the Rockefeller money in February 1968 and this provided salaries for Al, Bobby, Goat, J.W., and Dave. We were ready to move into our new office on April 4, 1968, the same day we held a press conference to announce the opening of Teen Town, and the day Martin Luther King, Jr. was killed. One day later the West Side burned.

We knew his death was trouble, and the night before the riot, the city was quiet, tense and waiting. A lot of the fellas wanted an excuse to start something; some were just ready if something jumped off; and others felt they wouldn't start anything, but they weren't going to stop anything that might start because the businessmen were going slow and had not thanked us for last summer.

The day after King's death, a Friday, the city made the mistake of not calling off school, so they had thousands of kids together that they couldn't control. The schools got hot and they had to let the kids out early. They started walking through the streets and when somebody broke the first window, the whole West Side was gone.

The riot started on Madison Street but later in the day, hundreds of young kids, none of them more than fifteen, walked down Sixteenth Street. Just after they passed the CVL office, the white drugstore on the corner where King had lived was on fire. After that, Larry's supermarket burned and then the streets belonged to the people. Although Mayor Daley had given the order to shoot to kill arsonists and shoot to maim looters, the police didn't try to stop anything; they just made a boundary for the riot. By the time the National Guard got there, there wasn't much happening.

On April 5, during the riot, Dave wrote down some of his observations:

> There are flames on Sixteenth and Hamlin; more flames on Sixteenth and Central Park. The street is dark but a glow of fire silhouettes shells of buildings. This is a riot—the emotional aftermath of the murder of Martin Luther King.
>
> After the assassination of John Kennedy, the country was stunned—but the shock was contained and the speculation that communists had plotted his death was not directed into overt acts. The death of JFK numbed the entire country—there was no one to fight, no target, no one to shoot at: the country was cool.
>
> The death of Martin Luther King was different; this was the death of a black leader. And though many street leaders did not like King while he lived, death by bullets was no way for a black man to die.

Throughout the immediate hours following King's death, the city was expectant — startled, confused, curious. No one knew what would happen. The city was worried and everyone knew just who to worry about.

Early in the evening of April 4, the FBI called Teen Town. I took the call and an agent said "what's happening?" He wanted the mood and he wanted a call if anything kicked off. We told him nothing was happening.

Chicago survived the first night but the news was just getting around. Some Saints wanted to know what the Lords would do, but the Lords were not talking and certainly were not preaching violence. Nevertheless, they were not telling people to be cool — not this time because there had been no thanks for last summer.

Friday morning the wires were alive with questions . . . the alderman, police, poverty officials — everybody was wondering. Then during the morning, the first reports came that windows were being broken on Madison; the news flashed that Washington, D.C., was in flames and the army had been ordered in: the riot had begun.

Word came that a group was coming down Sixteenth Street and Goat said they were coming our way. Within minutes, the group was on the corner and walking along the sidewalk in front of CVL headquarters. They were kids (few were over fourteen) and they were walking silently but purposefully. Store owners, and bystanders just watched and waited. Before long, somebody shouted that the drugstore was on fire. The riot was here. The kids had walked past black stores and hit the white drug store at Sixteenth and Hamlin. For the next hour the script was familiar: fire engines roared in; police blocked off the streets; and crowds gathered.

Inside the CVL office, I was restless, feeling cooped in. The fellas had warned me the night before that violence might break out and they had suggested I rent a room in the Loop until the shit was over. They warned me that somebody might break into my apartment just to shoot a honky — somebody who knew where I lived might spread the word that a honky was upstairs. Gut reaction told me to stay. If I had left, I would just have wondered what was happening on Sixteenth Street anyway. J.W. said nobody would feel that I was running, but of course I would have.

Finally Al asked if I wanted to go out (J.W. had repeatedly told me to keep my face out of the doorway so a trigger-happy stranger wouldn't see a white target). Anxious to get on the street, I loaded my camera, picked up a tape recorder, and with two Lords at my side and one to cover my back, I moved into the street.

The street was a carnival; some of the fellas were yelling "Vice Lawd!" and others handed out leaflets to start containing the action. Firefighters poured water on Larry's crumbling supermarket and the drug store just quietly burned. Helmeted riot police arrived in an unmarked car, but tonight the police were not moving, they were observers.

One brave little boy stepped up to Larry's big window and jumped in. He was quickly followed by a rushing crowd of kids falling over each other in a hurry to raid the shelves. Soon they reappeared with boxes of fruit, candy, and groceries. Police stood on the fringe. They knew, as did the audience of adults, that if they messed with any of those kids, the West Side would be gone. So far the destruction had been selective, but the entire city might go if a cop shot one of these young looters. The police strategy was containment. Stores were open and everything was on sale (a fire sale, you might say); there was not a damn thing the police could do.

We went to Sixteenth and Central park, two blocks from my apartment. While firefighters focused on one spot, we strode down the street with squads of younger Lords behind us. We stopped at the intersection. Suddenly, noises erupted from the crowd — a white man in a car. The crowd surrounded the old man and went for his car. Scared whiter than he was, the man pushed his foot to the floor. A crash of glass and I saw his window break as something hard bounced against my leg. The man escaped but he was a fool for driving through.

We watched the crowd, now noisy and cocky. One or two strangers came up and wondered who I was, but they were quickly informed that I belonged there. Bell was right, "Ain't nobody going to hurt you out here — people know you." What do you say when a man says he'll kill the motherfucker that touches you, and you know that he will? that even now, as I type in the glow of flames, Marquita and Shirley won't leave unless somebody stays to watch me. There I was — white, Ivy League, walking the centerline of Sixteenth Street, surrounded by rioting friends.

The riot had begun when schools released students early, but once the riot began, there were no questions, no doubts, no time to decide what side you're on. Just as Jackie had said, "we don't want this shit to break out, but if it does, we can't do anything to stop it," Sam agreed, "We'll be out there too." And they were.

There were two stores on the corner of Sixteenth and Central Park, one a drug store, the other a food store, both with iron grills in front of the windows, both owned by whites. The order was given: Break 'em in. A moment later the ironwork was ripped away and garbage cans crashed through the windows.

Black stores were untouched or only slightly damaged from breakage next door. Unprotected windows were unbroken while elsewhere iron grills were kicked in. Teen Town, the African Lion, planning office, and pool room were untouched, and there was no "soul brother" soaped on the windows. People knew who was who and who was where.

Yet with all the looting, breaking, and sirens, the street was orderly. People walked, strolled, and went about business like this was any other day. Violence was directed against property, not people, and the only danger was for whites.

There's no joy but there's a good feeling because in this riot there's integrity. Black people are standing up to The Man, and the medium is the message. The flames are tears for Martin Luther King and all black folk and the sirens are wails that whitey has fucked up because they killed the only man who was preaching non violence. But whites have not understood before so why will they now? Riots probably have outlived their value as an effective phase of a social revolution, but just as Martin Luther King refused to adjust to changing moods that demanded destruction, militants now are not adjusting to the hard reality that riots no longer accelerate improvement of the black man's condition. As with any people with a cause, the movement demands drama. But the work for black people today must be hard day-to-day organizing — the acquisition of economic and political power, a path that is usually tough, dull and routine.

When the riot ended, the fires had been worse than the great Chicago fire in 1871, and most of the white stores were no longer in the neighborhood. The Lords opened the office at 3720 West Sixteenth Street as a relief station and passed out food and clothing to more than three hundred families. All the fellas in the neighborhood helped even though some of them had been in the riot.

EDWARD V. HANRAHAN
State's Attorney of Cook County

All I see gangs doing is marauding, ravaging, shooting and killing.

1969

CAPTAIN EDWARD BUCKNEY
Gang Intelligence Unit, Chicago Police Department

If you can show me just one ounce of good they have done . . . then there might be something to say.

1968

They are hard-core criminals. They are not redeemable, and anybody who thinks they are is wasting his time.

1969

The Goat

We're trying to give government the answer if they would stop being so damn bullheaded.

1969

CONSERVATIVE VICE LORDS, INC.

3720 W. 16th St.

April 9, 1968

The Honorable Richard J. Daley
Mayor
City of Chicago
Chicago, Illinois

Dear Mayor Daley:

Conservative Vice Lords, Inc., is a non-profit corporation
chartered in September, 1967, to improve the social-economic
conditions of black people on the West Side of Chicago. We
represent 8,000-10,000 youth on the West Side.

The Chicago community knows us as a gang but we want the
people of Chicago to respect us as businessmen and concerned
citizens. Our efforts to earn this respect include the
proximate opening of "Teen Town," a restaurant to serve pri-
marily the teenagers, the "African Lion," an Afro-American
heritage shop, and a planning office. We have participated
in the creation, development, and direction of Operation
Bootstrap. Since last August, we have regularly attended meetings
of Bootstrap because we believe a coalition of businessmen and
clubs can do much to relieve problems in Lawndale.

Since becoming incorporated, we have received a $15,000 planning
grant from the Rockefeller Foundation matched by $15,000 from
Operation Bootstrap. We consider these grants an investment
in our hopes to change our image. We are attempting to direct
the misspent energies of streetfighting to the constructive
development of social and economic programs to serve our members
and the community of Lawndale.

But as the riot of these last few days illustrates, discontent
cuts deep into the black community and social programs have
not reached the street. Social programs so far have sacrificed
honest and effective efforts for superficial calm. As reported
in a federal study entitled, "From The Street," for which some
of our members conducted interviews last summer, many young
people and almost all the persons considered "hard core" are
untouched by government programs.

We are the street so we did not need this report to know what
programs have been ineffective in involving the hard core.
We are some of the discontent whose feelings sometimes are

expressed violently because there is no other way to express
them. Yet we also are an organization that proposes now to work
for constructive change.

In the last few days, we were on the street urging young people
to end the burning and looting that had started as almost a
spontaneous wail from within the black ghetto; we distributed
3000 hand bills telling our brothers to be cool and to honor
our dead brother with the non-violence that he preached; and
we organized an emergency relief service for families either
burned out or in desperate need of help. We have passed out
food and clothing from our headquarters to more than three
hundred families.

But these efforts are simply first-aid for the crisis of these
few days. We are concerned more with what must be done to prevent
future disorders; with efforts that must be made to restore
hope to black people; and with work that must be started to
solve the economic plight of our community. We feel that this
effort must be directed from within the community itself; we
feel that we should control programs that are intended for us and
we should own shares in our community. Conservative Vice Lords,
Inc., asks your personal help in beginning the effort which
for us must be a sustained day-to-day fight. We are prepared
to fight the problems of urban reconstruction just as hard as
we used to fight among ourselves on the street. We need your help.

Specifically, we ask you to do the following:

     1. Appoint a liaison from your office who would work with
us on problems between our organization and the city government
and who would be responsible directly to you.

     2. We are submitting a proposal to Vista for a summer
program involving 25 Vista Associates. We would like your
endorsement of this program.

     3. During the summer, we would like to organize a
beautification program. We need 110 Neighborhood Youth Corps
workers under the direction of CVL, Inc. We would also like
to borrow the necessary equipment from the Department of
Sanitation - this includes a Department of Sanitation truck
available for daily removal of rubbish that we collect.
We would like cooperation from the Chicago Park District in
the form of providing earth, grass seed, flower seed, and
fertilizer.

4. We hope to obtain motion picture equipment and feature films which we will show each night in five different neighborhoods in our community. We need two hundred portable chairs to provide seats for these shows.

5. We have a list of several vacant lots. We would like lots in our neighborhood deeded to CVL, Inc., so that we can run them ourselves as totlots.

6. We will be developing many proposals. We want you to evaluate these proposals, and if you judge them sound, to be personally responsible for finding money that will fund them on our terms. We will not accept middlemen. We want money to be transferred from the original source to us. We will hire accountants but we must have authority to hire and fire everyone in the program. We need your help in developing relationships that make this possible.

We know that a personal interest by you can do much to expedite the implementation of our ideas. We also know that these are the terms under which programs must be established if programs are to reach the unreached. And we know that unless these unreached become involved, the discontent which has been burned into our memory will not cease.

The federal report, "From The Street," recommended that youth be involved in the planning and operation of summer programs. We are the rejected youth of Lawndale, and we ask your help in making this recommendation a reality.

                                        Alfonso Alford
                                        President.

Who But the Lord?
By Langston Hughes

I looked and I saw
That man they call the Law,
He was coming
Down the street at me!
I had visions in my head
Of being laid out cold and dead,
Or else murdered
By the third degree.
    I said, O, Lord, if you can,
    Save me from that man!
    Don't let him make a pulp out of me!
    But the Lord he was not quick,
    The Law raised up his stick
    And beat the living hell
    Out of me!
Now I do not understand
Why God don't protect a man
From police brutality.
Being poor and black,
I've no weapon to strike back
So who but the Lord
Can protect me?
    We'll see.

An Ounce of Good

We had some damn good riots, but then we looked around and began building. We had the office and some money and in the next two years, 1968 through 1969, we developed programs that demonstrated the pride that black people must feel to free themselves from the fatalistic feeling that nothing can be done, the resignation that life cannot be changed, and the despair that nobody cares.

CVL awakened fellows on the street to the dream of something new. We give a cat a taste of something better in life and show him ways to get it. As Alfonso has said:

"Like society itself, we are in a time of change. Just as we used to fight each other on the street, we now stand together in a different fight for life — the life of a city, the life of a neighborhood and the life of a people who have been declared unemployable, uneducable, and unreached."

In 1968 and 1969 we developed many programs.

TEEN TOWN:

With funds from Alderman Collins and Sears Roebuck, we converted a once gutted storefront into a first-class ice cream parlor with wall paneling and sparkling equipment. We had problems with bookkeeping, but on a corner that the Chicago *Sun-Times* described as having "more problems for a square block than any other in the city," we opened an air-conditioned restaurant that seats twenty-seven people.

THE AFRICAN LION:

To encourage pride in black history and to expose black residents of the West Side to the rich heritage of Africa, CVL created the African Lion, a soul shop to sell clothing and accessories.

With a grant from the Field Foundation of Illinois, the directors of the African Lion, Bill Stevenson and Eddie Harris, designed a business training program for

126

the employees and CVL emphasized that the development of an Afro-American identity for Black Americans should not be considered a separatist movement but rather a people's search for meaning.

Most of the ethnic groups that settled the United States have clung to the heritage of their ancestors. We believe that the development of respect for an African heritage will offer a sense of pride and dignity that will prepare black people to deal more adequately with the degradation, discrimination and exploitation that are part of daily life in the ghetto.

In a brochure we printed as a financial annual "Report to the Public," we said that "the extent to which black people can cope with ghetto life and fight to eradicate the sickness that perpetuates ghetto conditions is the extent to which our whole society will have the strength to realize the dreams we all share."

TASTEE FREEZ:

Tastee Freez was a business that we hoped would help to sustain our non-income-producing programs. The American National Bank approved a loan and we opened one franchise at 1801 South Pulaski and another at 703 South California under the Kedzie, Albany and Terrible Vice Lords.

Not all our efforts succeeded, however, and eventually both locations were closed. Our loan had been enough to lease the equipment and open the doors but not enough for working capital. There was too much work for the manager, not enough time for training, and too little money to keep us above water until the business could get going. White businesses sometimes don't expect to break even for a few years, but the bankers didn't tell us we might need more money.

SIMONE:

Simone was a business venture with Sammy Davis Jr., and this was CVL's biggest business failure. We spent almost a year developing a distribution system for cosmetics made particularly for black skin. We had an offlce and training for people who would sell Simone door to door like Avon, but Simone never did more than manufacture sample products. This was a blow to us because we could have been working on other programs.

WEST SIDE COMMUNITY DEVELOPMENT CORPORATION:

CVL joined four other groups to form an economic coalition. These were the Garfield Organization, West Side Organization, Student Afro-American Group, and Egyptian Cobras.

The first business was the West Side Paper Stock Company which was financed by the First National Bank of Chicago and developed with the Container Corporation of America.

As one of the five groups in WSCDC, CVL received a cash award at the conference of the Strategy for the New City: 1969-1972 "for its emerging role in establishing a strong economic and political community in the New City. The West Side Community Development Corporation was commended because represented in it are five organizations that have rejected old rivalries and banded together because they recognize the root of the community's problem as economic."

MANAGEMENT TRAINING INSTITUTE:

The Coalition for Youth Action in the U.S. Department of Labor funded a twenty week program that taught black history, self-awareness, reading, and business skills such as banking, business correspondence, and salesmanship.

This training was an investment in the future of the community because it prepared twenty young Lords and Ladies to direct CVL programs.

STREET ACADEMY:

The emphasis in the Management Training Institute on the development of identity and aspiration led to the opening of a street academy for high school dropouts. This was a way for young people to catch up on their education without leaving the community. By a cooperative arrangement with Malcolm X Community College, there was also a way to continue education beyond high school.

PARTNERS:

In 1968 the Ford Foundation gave $130,000 to improve the executive skills of CVL Inc. leaders. In an experimental coalition an officer of CVL Inc. was the director in each of four divisions: administration, training, new enterprises, and neighborhood action, and a young professional was assigned as Partner director. The Vice Lords would direct and decide and the Partners would consult and advise.

Through this grant, CVL began the development of several programs and came into close contact with many people in the white community. But the grant was for only one year and this was not enough time to define new roles, develop new programs and at the same time hold the street together.

THE HOUSE OF LORDS:

With our own money, we opened two neighborhood "hang-ins" especially for young people under eighteen—young brothers and sisters who have no place but the street. One was with the City Lords and another with the Homan and Fifteenth Lords.

In our announcement of the opening of the House of Lords we said, "The House of Lords is open free to everyone in the neighborhood. We will have card tables, ping pong, game machines, jukebox and books (get hip to what black power really means!). This is your place—sleep, study, dance, stay warm in the winter." We offered to find tutors for anybody who wanted one and we got books from several publishers.

BEAUTIFICATION

The first summer program (1968) was an example of "Inreach," our idea to involve the youth that society had rejected. We did not have to reach out as many institutions must. We simply had to reach in because we are them. We did not have to spend time gaining rapport with the street corner society because we had been brothers of the street since we were born.

We knew that the city was supposed to keep our streets clean and pick up the garbage, but the city was not doing the job. Unless we wanted to live in filth until

"CLEAN UP - PAINT UP - FIX UP - TO SHAPE UP"

We The Conservative Lords are planning to further improve the LAWNDALE AREA. As you have noticed, we have planted grass and cleaned up the corners of 16th Street. We would like to continue this in the areas of 15th Street through 18th Streets. We need your support to better our communities. As parents, owners and businessmen of this area, we ask that you help us by:

1. Cleaning up the litter in front and back of your homes and establishments.

2. Supervise your children.
   Teach them to help keep it clean, and not tear it up.

3. Throw trash in "Trash Cans" "Not on sidewalks".

4. Please keep your kids out of the grass when it is planted.

HELP US TO MAKE YOURS A BETTER PLACE TO LIVE.

Thank You,

Conservative Vice Lords

For information call - 762-9279
Ask for Al, Bobby, or J. W.

We the Conservative Vice Lords are asking for your support. There are many new apartment buildings being erected in our community. These buildings are yours, and the need for more of them is great so that everyone can have a chance to live in decent surroundings for a change.

We are asking you as parents to supervise the children who are hampering the completion of these sites. Two buildings, one at 1526 Millard, the other on the corner of 15th and Millard, have been damaged by children who:

    1. Play on equipment that could cause serious injury.

    2. Destroy valuable materials.

    3. Build small fires on the new floors.

    4. Tear out newly-installed electrical wiring.

    5. Threaten the workers.

    6. Remove materials from the sites and throw them up and down the streets and allies.

This must stop immediately if we are to change our standards of living. If every parent could supervise his own child, our problems would cease to be.

We the Conservative Vice Lords are committed to watch these sites and we are going to see to it that they are completed without any further interruptions.

We all, as community people, will benefit by their completions which will give some of us better living conditions.

Thank you,
Conservative Vice Lords Inc.
3720 W. 16th St.
521-9745

the city could be forced to give us service, we had to do something ourselves.

Under the slogan "Where there was glass, there will be grass," we got one hundred Neighborhood Youth Corps positions from the Catholic School Board and an administrative grant from the Field Foundation of Illinois. With Glenn Smith as director, we spent the summer sweeping streets, picking up trash, and planting grass.

TENANTS' RIGHTS ACTION GROUP:

Many landlords issued illegal scare warnings and notices to evict tenants. Most tenants did scare and failed to realize that the notices were illegal. Sometimes a person even found himself on the street with his furniture, not knowing why or what to do.

The CVL housing service under Percy Williams was available free to help people with these problems. The people around Sixteenth Street knew that if they brought these problems to CVL, we would be on the case. Our record was:

43 illegal evictions blocked
11 court victories
0 court defeats
32 families relocated

ART & SOUL:

Art & Soul began as a six-month art happening in Lawndale by the Sesquicentennial Commission and continued under CVL with a grant from the Weiboldt Foundation and assistance from the University of Illinois, Circle Campus. The idea was developed by CVL and Jan van der Marck of the Museum of Contemporary Art.

With neighborhood carpenters, electricians and plumbers, CVL converted two unoccupied storefronts into a studio and gallery. Just as the museum was reaching people by moving beyond the confines of brick and mortar, CVL stimulated the unrecognized talent of dropouts, "delinquents," and winos.

Jackie Hetherington and Don McIlvaine were directors, and there was an advisory board that included members from the Museum of Contemporary Art, the Art Institute of Chicago, the Chicago Public Library, the Lawndale Youth Commission, and the Lawndale Peoples Planning and Action Conference.

Anyone could just walk in and paint and there was also free instruction. There was an artist in residence program, a writers' workshop, and to take art to the community Don McIlvaine made two street murals, one a half block long at Art & Soul and another two stories high behind Teen Town.

EVENTS:

There were bus trips to baseball games, the zoo, and the theater to see Sammy Davis in Golden Boy, and on every holiday, CVL organized a celebration for the neighborhood. On the Fourth of July there were barbecues on the sidewalk, and at Christmas there was a dinner in the poolroom.

On Christmas, Al got neighborhood merchants to contribute turkey, cranberries, vegetables, potatoes and liquor, and several ladies volunteered to cook. The pool tables were covered and radiators that usually cooked the beans on cold nights kept the dinner warm.

Everybody was invited, and people even sent kids with plates to take something home. About seventy people came to eat. Big Carl gave out free reefers, and the jukebox got everybody down for a soulful Black Christmas.

DIRECT ACTION:

CVL worked with Operation Breadbasket and the Reverend Jesse Jackson to protest welfare cuts and get food for the hungry and joined a coalition to make the trade unions and the construction industry stop discrimination against blacks.

In the summer of 1969, CVL joined the Coalition for United Community Action to stop over $100 million of construction. With LSD (Lords, Stones, and Disciples) in the vanguard, the Coalition stopped construction until the unions negotiated a plan to let blacks in the trades.

The way the construction industry discriminates is to let blacks mix mortar, carry sandbags or take bricks to the bricklayers—just enough tokenism so they can say they put a few niggers on the job. There is no promotion and blacks have no control over construction in black communities.

During the demonstrations, there was no opposition as long as we were closing sites in the black community. But at Circle Campus of the University of Illinois, we were getting too close to the Loop so the police started to bust heads.

The first week we had a nonviolent demonstration. Nobody got out of line and nobody put his hands on any of the workers or the equipment; we just asked for cooperation in closing down the sites and we showed them the list of demands we had. We wanted blacks to be put in the trades as apprentices so with Model Cities coming in, there would be black cats ready to work.

When we got to the university, the police said we were out of our neighborhood. There was some violence as the police busted heads, but then SCLC brought in the ladies and babies and eventually the unions negotiated.

The Chicago Plan promised four thousand jobs and the first thousand were supposed to go to LSD. But these were jobs for people with high school diplomas, not for the fellas who had done the marching. We were supposed to have jobs and we set up a recruiting center, but when fellas were sent to apply, they got a long story and came back with no job.*

---

* On October 23, 1989, on the 20th anniversary of the Minority Construction agreement, Bobby Gore received an award "for representing his organization in demonstrations, strategy development and negotiations for the Chicago Plan."

Remembered as "the year that made the difference," when black community leaders and contractors took a stand for jobs, an anniversary commitee of black contractors presented awards to a long list of elected officials and community leaders — awards that ranged from the Rev. C.T. Vivien to posthumous appreciation to Mayor Richard J. Daley for spending "over 110 hours of his personal time in working to negotiate differences between the Black Coalition and the Trade Unions and majority contractors."

In explaining the awards, Paul King, chairman of the anniversary committee, said that "ingratitude is the greatest of all sins," but in the citations, King and his committee didn't have the courage to name the gangs that made this anniversary possible. They seemed more interested in getting close to the new Mayor Daley than honoring truth in history.

Although every other award identified organizational affiliations, the awards to Gore, spokesman for the Vice Lords and Leonard Sengali, spokesman for the Black P Stones, didn't mention by name the vanguard known as LSD—Lords, Stones and Disciples. In the discrete language of

YOUTH ORGANIZATIONS UNITED:

Y.O.U. is a national coalition of youth groups which was formed to provide a platform to discuss ideas, programs, resources and the experiences of street groups throughout the country.

Early in 1968 the Department of Labor funded a program for developing communications among youth groups. The idea started with The Real Great Society in New York, and CVL assumed responsibility for contacting groups in the Midwest. Four Lords were employed fulltime for two months to talk with groups and invite them to a conference in East St. Louis, Illinois.

There were over fifty groups and three hundred people at the conference. The organizations included The Young Great Society in Philadelphia, the Mission Rebels from San Francisco, Leeway Inc., from Chinatown, San Francisco; The Way Inc., Minneapolis; Thugs United, New Orleans; and the Brown Berets and Sons of Watts in Los Angeles.

Warren Gilmore, a member of CVL Inc., was elected national president, and Doc Brown, another Lord, was elected regional vice president. Gilmore opened a national office in Washington and has been working there since the conference.

Lelan F. Sillin, Jr., president of Northeast Utilities, described Y.O.U. as "offering constructive alternatives to help build on the basic values of our society. Ours is the opportunity to show that we will respond to such alternatives, and that to act we do not have to be prodded by threats made to our institutions."

These programs create a sense of identity that street cats are looking for. There is a sense of control, a sense of ownership.

We're doing something where a guy can actually step out the front door and make a decent living, and he doesn't have to spend a big proportion of his money getting back and forth to work. Most of the employment now is in suburban towns and the average person works a whole week for ninety dollars and then turns around and spends nine dollars of that on the guy he's riding with.

Like Cupid says, "Right now, we're doing everything we can to create jobs so we won't have to go out to Skokie or to Elks Grove or some place like that. We're trying to create jobs here that will pay a living salary for us, the people in the community. I don't feel we should go out to Elks Grove or different places. I don't feel we should go out there 'cause we ain't doin' nothin' but helping them. I feel it's time for us to help ourselves and by helping ourselves we have to create jobs to bring money to the community. Then we can bring our people back out of Elks Grove and different suburbs where most Negroes work . . . and

bourgeois cowards, the committee singled out the spokesmen of these gangs "for representing his organization."

They had embraced gangs in 1969 when they closed construction sites, but twenty years later, gang names were deleted from the record while Mayor Daley, The Boss who's stranglehold had to be broken, was resurrected with full honors.

when I say Negroes, I mean Uncle Toms. The black people is right here.''

Bobby quit fulltime work as a butcher to help change the conditions that made his father work for forty-five cents an hour at a job he had to take.

''Now he's been out on the job thirty-six years and ain't got nothin' comin'. We've been wasting generations of people and the only way we can live decent and stop all the beggin', the rapin', the dope fiends and the pocketbook snatchin' is to get an economic base here and create enough jobs for people to do their own thing in building the community. This gives them pride and prestige in the community.

''By sitting back and looking, we found out that if you don't have money, you don't do anything. Money is the power structure. Money makes people sit down and listen to you. This means not only jobs but ownership. Like this cat Louis Kelso in San Francisco says, we got to own what this country produces and not depend just on gettin' jobs.

''When we get our thing together, we won't have to step over garbage and filth and shit gettin' out of our own house to go take care of somebody else's garbage and filth and shit. Right now, 5 per cent of the people control about 80 per cent of the economy. If we had the money that some of these cats spend just getting somebody to count their money, then we would have some changes.''

We have worked on plans for a gas station, a roller skating rink, a day care center, a neighborhood park, and several other ideas. None of these has worked out. But many doors have been opened and many iron bars have been ripped off vacant storefront windows to show the young brothers that we can build up the community.

We have a number of people that we're trying to get to because they want the street to make a living for them and the street can't make a living for them. You would think that the routine on the street would make a guy want to go to school and learn just that much harder. But some people just don't want to learn; some are just too cool to learn, and others feel what's the use of going to school: ''Look at you; what did you get out of it?''

A kid does not go back to school until he finds a reason why. The reason he dropped out is because there is no reason to stay. Like when Goat was a kid they told stories about Little Black Sambo. ''Why the hell should I sit in a hot classroom and listen to stories about a little colored kid running around a tree and a bunch of tigers following

him. We're going to the moon and they're still teaching Little Black
Sambo. A cat grow up on the street and at the age of fifteen he's almost
grown. He's not gonna read Dick run, Sally watch Dick run.''

The little that kids do learn cannot even be applied in Lawndale so
the goal of CVL is to open up the community so a cat can come out
of high school and if he wants to be a CPA, he can go to college and
work right here.

The way things are now the average cat that comes out of high school
and has some fat around the brain feels that he has to get away: there's
no middle class in Lawndale.

Since the assassination of King, even before that, black people have
become aware of what we're up against, and we know the fight is not
among ourselves but with the outside. We were always taught not to
trust and have confidence in each other. We were taught to believe our
own brothers were out to get us, and any time a brother spoke against
abuse, he was rebelling against white society.

There has been a complete feeling of hopelessness in our neighborhood.
Guys don't really have any ambition; they don't have any get up and
go. They don't think things are open to them, and to an extent things
are not open. A few years ago Bobby felt this way.

"I felt, well, what the hell; I'll never learn anything, I'll never be
nobody. But rather than run from the problem, you stay and fight with
the problem and try to get your composure back. You get your pride.

"We're trying to stop the running and see what we can come up with
right here. There are many ways that you can get to a cat. Some will
change fast — you rap some and you can tell that you're gettin' to his
heart — and he begins to show a different attitude. But then we got some
Vice Lords out here that are wrong.

"If we catch some of these teenage leaders and they want to kill some
honkies, break windows, snatch pocketbooks or rape, we talk with them.
Now we cannot change a person's mind, but we can create some things
that will happen around him so that eventually he will have to change
his attitude.

"But we can't blame them. We blame the system. We blame the
environment. We blame the things that they had to grow up around
and in.

"We got cats out here that have never had a chance to think for
themselves, and they're sixteen, seventeen years old. There's always
been somebody to tell them how they should think, but there comes a
time when you're supposed to think what you want to think.

"The schools should try and give the kids something to say about how the school should be run rather than to come in with their own curriculum and say you follow this. Let the kids have a part in what's to be said and what's to be done.

"You got to give a cat a chance to use his mind. The worse thing you can do is go tell a guy to do this or do that. The only people that these cats are going to relate to is a gang set. Or it's gonna be some white folks comin' in tellin' these kids to do this or do that for a few bucks.

"Now some guys present themselves in a fashion where I have had to punch some of them in the eye—simply because I tried to tell him that he wasn't doing himself any good. . . a cat's standing up here actually killing himself and don't know it. Then when you try and pull his coat to it, make him aware, then he wants to put his dukes up or run and get a gun. But he'll listen to somebody that comes from the outside somewhere; he'll listen to all this crap and he'll go away grinnin'. Here I growed up with the cat, been together fifteen years in the same neighborhood, and when I try and tell him that he's wrong and to think for himself, then right away we gotta have some harsh words and he's gonna get a pistol. . . which is going to make me go get one.

"Right now they're asleep, and like those white college kids are trying to do, we have to wake up everybody. Not just the cat on the street but the neighborhood and the government so they will hear what we are talking about. Why do we live like we do and why aren't we better off than we really are? Why do we have to fight in Vietnam when the real fight is here on Sixteenth Street? If we had guys like Rap Brown or Stokely Carmichael or the guys talking about awareness, then maybe we wouldn't have turned out the way we did. Rap opened a lot of eyes, and you can't discredit any guy that's out there talking about black awareness, whether that's violence or whatever. Everybody's doing his own thing and eventually we'll become one thing.

"We're dealing with all the people. We got some cats up in the crowd who give you sleepless nights because all they need is a chance. Even though the Mayor thinks we're just a bunch of hoodlums, Dave recorded the voices of three different Vice Lords who speak for what we're trying to do."

ANDRE

"My name is Andre and I'm eleven years old."
"Are you a Vice Lord, Andre?"
"Yes."

"Why?"

"Because lots of my friends are in the Vice Lords."

"What do you do as a Vice Lord?"

"I go on trips and go to Springfield*. . . come in the office and see if anybody needs any help."

"What kind of member are you?"

"I'm just an ordinary member."

"What branch are you in?"

"I'm a young enforcer."

"What do you want to be when you grow up?"

"A Vice Lord."

"Why?"

"Because ever since I've been little I've been a Vice Lord, and I'm going to grow up and be a Vice Lord."

"When did you become a Vice Lord?"

"When I was around five years old."

"How many of your friends are Vice Lords?"

"I'd say around fifty."

"What do you want to do as a Vice Lord when you grow up?"

"I want to help the hungry and try to clean up the neighborhood . . . stop kids from throwin' bottles and breakin' in stores."

"How much money do you want to make?"

"I ain't worryin' about the money. I'm just worryin' about the other people."

DUKE

"I'm thirty-four. I'm not a thirty-four-year-old man that hasn't grown up. I have a girlfriend my same age; I have one kid, she has two.

Now, it's a little difficult to tell another thirty-four-year-old person that you're a Vice Lord. Most people refer to Vice Lords as a street gang—nothing beneficial comes out, only fights, cuttin', and shootin'—and as far as they are concerned, this is what I associate myself with.

"But the Vice Lords are not made up of just plain streetfighters any more. Most people are surprised to see the Vice Lords with a planning office, telephone, desk, swivel chairs, and typewriters. To them, this doesn't exist. So when a person reads that the police department is

* The State Capital of Illinois.

declaring war on gangs to stop these hoodlums, they feel that you are a member of that hoodlum action that the city is going to stop. They don't associate you with a typewriter and desk and telephone. They don't associate you with Teen Town or a place where needy people can come and get help.

"They don't associate you with nothin' like that. All your good deeds are overshadowed by the general impression. But, believe me, if this were a hoodlum gang and I had to fight with everybody that's across the street, and I couldn't leave here without four or five more Vice Lords to see me home, I wouldn't be part of this. I work everyday and I don't have time for it.

"I get no money from the Vice Lords because I'm not on any of the programs. I give my wife time in the evenings after work and I go down to the CVL office at my convenience.

"A thirty-four-year-old man with the Vice Lords is nothing. It's no more for me to be a Vice Lord than it would be for a white fella out North to say that I'm thirty-four-years-old and I belong to a lodge. I'm a lodge member. He goes to his lodge meetings and he pays his dues and that doesn't mean he's not a responsible father and husband and doesn't pay his house note and his car note.

"It's the same way with me. This is my lodge, that's all. I associate myself with the youngsters, but it's to an extent, not to an extreme. The youngsters around here, they call me by name; I call them by name. They're Lords and they know I'm a Lord."

RICHARD

"This is open-the-door Richard talkin'. I don't know if I'll be able to talk again. I'm goin' on fifty-four years old.

"I seen a lotta goin' on and a lotta fightin' and robbin'. I have been beat up a lotta times on this street; I only lucky I ain't been killed. I have been stabbed in my back clean through to my third rib.

"They was bad then. They was knockin' people in the head, robbin' and stealin', and soon as you shoot a five- or ten-dollar bill out there on the street, they take it away from you. And if you walk down the street in the dark, you don't got a chance. If you go under a light, they won't bother you. They wait 'til you get drunk and then they beat you up.

"Now I want to say this. These boys over here in Lawndale don't do nothin' to nobody. They, don't steal, they don't rob. These boys are tryin' to keep this place clean, and all these boys here got this office, this place of business, and everywhere they keep it clean. The boys are runnin' it and I hope God will bless 'em and bless every place on these streets.

"Mayor Daley, wherever you at and wherever you be, we out here to help our own self. We have to try to help our own self. You don't try to help us. We want peace in this here Chicago. Let us live and be happy, regardless of the race or color. We got to love one another. We got to fight for our freedom and live with one another and die with one another, not hate. That's what I want."

Collage of clippings by *Jody Ginsberg*

W. Side Gang Starts A Self-Help Program

By Basil Talbott Jr.

A West Side Youth gang which chartered itself as a not-for-profit organization announced Wednesday it is beginning a neighborhood self-help program funded by private sources.

First enterprise of the group, the Conservative Vice Lords Inc., will be a teen center at 3700 W. 16th, said Bobby Gore, spokesman for CVL.

A $15,000 grant from the Rockefeller Foundation and $15,000 from Operation bootstrap will be used as seed money to develop the community-wide effort, Gore said.

Gore told a press conference at the new center, Teen Town, the money will finance the hiring of four CVL members as planners and another as secretary.

Some of the funds were used to employ the Trans Century Corp. of Washington, D.C., as a consultant "in program development and management," Gore said.

CVL obtained a state charter on its own last September and will open offices at the Teen Town address.

Representatives of many of the 26 segments of the lords, as well as their president, Alfonso Alfrid, attended the press conference.

Businesses expected to open soon include The African Lion, an Afro-American heritage shop at 3749 W. 16th, and an employment center.

"We welcome the help of industry, government or any organization, but all CVL programs must be CVL-owned and-managed," Gore said. "We are the grass roots people. We know who needs help and we can get help to them

where others have failed."

As in the past, Gore said, the Lords will urge troublemakers to stay out of the area.

"We want the West Side to be the best side," he said. "We're not going to let anybody take over. We're going to run the West Side."

Echoing the Swahili slogan for courage, Gore left this message for Lawndale youth: "Zena Zena Bu."

CHICAGO SUN-TIMES, Thurs., Apr. 4, 1968

The Conservative Vice Lords outside their West Side teen center. (Sun-Times Photo)

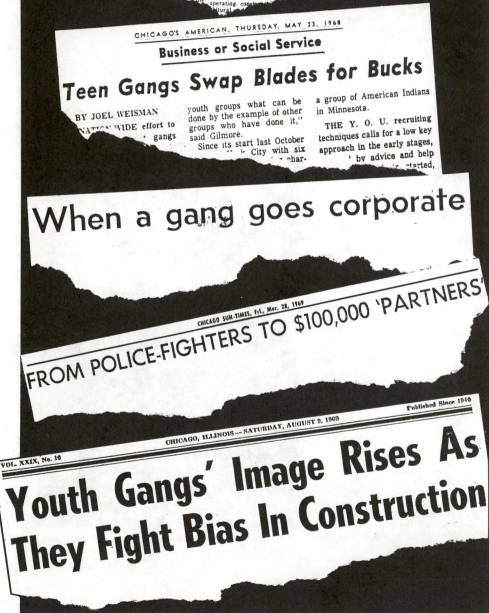

'We're No Gang,' Members Of The Vice Lords Assert

Members of the Conservative Vice Lords, Inc., declaring their intention to "take the bottom of our bag, turn it up side down and shock people all over the world with some of the positive changes we can make," no longer be classified as a for the CVL

ber of CVL who was recently voted president of the nationally organized Y.O.U., Inc., said he also wanted it made clear that the youth organization is not a teenage mafia. He said: "Y.O.U. is an alliance, non-profit and legally incorporated organization of established youth groups throughout the United States. The primary sponsors of Y.O.U. are operating const

development of new youth groups in other cities."

He added that the organization is designed to give youth groups "an alternative to re-volution.

"Our country has suffered from urban disorder and many people are searching for ways to reconstruct society. Y.O.U. is a soluti

CHICAGO'S AMERICAN, THURSDAY, MAY 23, 1968

Business or Social Service

Teen Gangs Swap Blades for Bucks

BY JOEL WEISMAN

NATIONWIDE effort to gangs

youth groups what can be done by the example of other groups who have done it," said Gilmore.

Since its start last October City with six char-

a group of American Indians in Minnesota.

THE Y. O. U. recruiting techniques calls for a low key approach in the early stages, by advice and help started,

When a gang goes corporate

CHICAGO SUN-TIMES, Fri., Mar. 28, 1969

FROM POLICE-FIGHTERS TO $100,000 'PARTNERS'

Published Since 1940

CHICAGO, ILLINOIS — SATURDAY, AUGUST 9, 1969

VOL. XXIX, No. 10

Youth Gangs' Image Rises As They Fight Bias In Construction

Street Gangs Turn a Profit on Their Brand of Violence

**BY WILLIAM JONES
AND JOSEPH BOYCE**

In the midst of a Senate investigation last year into a $972,000 war on poverty scandal involving the Blackstone Rangers street gang, Ranger leaders were approached by a national magazine.

The publication wanted to do an article on the day-to-day activities of the Rangers, including a comprehensive picture layout.

Ask $25,000 in Cash

"Fine," said the leaders.

They asked $25,000 in cash for the article, 2 per cent of the gross receipts from the issue in which it appeared, and $150-a-week salaries for a number of Ranger bodyguards to accompany reporters and photographers. The magazine rejected the proposal and the article was never written.

The incident shows that in the last several years some of Chicago's largest street gangs have become big business. They have discovered that vast sources of revenue made available by government agencies and private foundations do not include the risks connected with vice operations or extortion from merchants.

In the case of the Conservative Vice Lords, the largest gang in the Lawndale community, such grants have totaled $221,000 since the beginning of 1968.

The Rangers have enjoyed a $50,000 foundation grant for bail bonds and legal defense and were the only street gang to receive salaries in a scandal-ridden $972,000 war on poverty program that employed high school dropouts as program supervisors and instructors.

Sgt. Julius Frazier of the police gang intelligence unit puts it this way:

Alfonso Alford

David Dawley

"These gang leaders aren't stupid. They found out that hooliganism under a well-publicized name brought in vast amounts of money from public and private sources. The big money kept the older teenagers in t h e organization longer. Under normal circumstances they would have graduated from street shootings to a job in their late teens. But now you see the leaders of these gangs in their 20s and 30s."

Pay for Responsibility

The leader of the Vice Lords is Alfonso Alford, 34, of 1502 Ridgeway av., a former construction worker and pool hall operator, who now directs the operations of the gang-financed Teen Town restaurant at 3700 16th st.

But Alford is not considered the key to the gang's success in obtaining more than $200,000 in less than two years.

The expertise in applying for funds belongs to David Dawley, a white advisor and salaried employe who lives at 1611 S. Lawndale av. Dawley first met gang leaders last year when he was employed by the Trans-Century corporation to evaluate the attitudes of inner city youths for summer work programs. He quit the corporation to work with the gang but refused to disclose his salary.

Grants Fund Businesses

"We feel a guy should be paid commensurate with the level of his responsibility and at a level comparable to someone in a similar situation in business or industry," said Dawley. "They [gang leaders] make decisions involving businesses; employes, and even fellows on the street."

Since joining the gang payroll, D a w l e y has obtained grants of $25,000 from the Field foundation, $15,000 from the Rockefeller foundation, a n d $15,000 from Operation Bootstrap, a program sponsored by industry and business. He also wrote the proposals which resulted in grants of $130,000 from the Ford foundation and $36,000 from the department of labor.

Dawley describes his employers as "not a gang, but a serious company, going about economic development."

CHICAGO TRIBUNE

POLICE SHOWN SHOPS, CLUBS OF VICE LORDS

Former Street Gang Holds 'Open House'

BY BARRY POLSKY

The Conservative Vice Lords and the police mixed it again yesterday on the side.

But instead of t
ith knives

[CHICAGO'S AMERICAN Photo]

BOBBY GORE, vice president of the Vice Lords, chats with Sgt. Robert Tabor during open house for police.

BUT NOT ALL TUNE IN

Police Get a Peek at 'New Look' Image of Black Vice Lords

BY DOROTHY STORCK

THEY MIGHT HAVE BEEN THE Boy Scouts of America. They weren't, of course. Different kind of merit badges. A soul brother handshake instead of a salute.

But the organized vigor was vaguely familiar. Like a black comedy take-off of the Badger Troop Thanksgiving jamboree.

The Conservative Vice Lords Inc., were having an open For the cops. It was a master stroke of public re-

completely disarming, wildly funny, utterly

bed on the soft underbelly of his civic
react the way he always does at

d cop, and said "My,
arresting

CHICAGO TRIBUNE

Nearly 200 Street Gangs Roam Every City Area

Meeting Held at East St. Louis

National Ghetto Youth Group Is Organized

A Move Toward Understanding

The Conservative Vice Lords, whose name betrays their origins as one of the city's many tough street gangs, have invited members of the Chicago police department to tea—or at least to an open house tomorrow at three of the Lord's establishments.

The invitation itself is a hopeful sign. It is aimed at "changing attitudes and developing understanding."

And so is the response from Marquette District commander William A. McCann. He said, "We need new ideas and activities for working toward better relationships between citizens and the police."

The innocuous sounding little social would have been unthinkable five years ago because of attitudes and activities on both sides. All too often organizations in the city's black communities have opposed all policemen, on the grounds that they were callous outsiders, while the great majority of residents feared crime in their neighborhoods and urgently desired more police protection. And all too often, police officials have viewed any independent organization in the black community as a challenge to constituted authority and a threat to the peace.

We hope tomorrow's social affair will be a start toward breaking down these barriers of mutual suspicion.

CHICAGO SUN-TIMES   EDITORIAL PAGE

EX-YOUTH GANG INVITES POLICE TO OPEN HOUSE

Vice Lords Open Teen 'Hang-In'

The Conservative Vice Lords Inc., announced the opening of a neighborhood "hang in," a center of recreation for youngsters under 18 years of age, at 3722 W. 16th st.

Called, "The House of Lords", the center is attracting some 50 to 100 children who play ping-pong, game machines, card games a jukebox curfew.

According to Alfonso CVL, president, study and books will be shortly. The center vote a quiet hou

"Many of the ters do not to study or read by,"

"The fun br

CHICAGO SUN-TIMES, Tues., Feb. 24, 1970

Street gangs growth told

CHICAGO DAILY NEWS, Wednesday, July 10

Rangers and Vice Lords call for peace, slum improvement

Vice Lords To Battle Slum Housing

CHICAGO SUN-TIMES

Ask public aid in war on gangs

At press conference Monday to discuss the war on gangs are (l. to r.) Sta V. Hanrahan, Mayor Daley, Police Supt. James B. Conlisk Jr., and Fire Comr

Conservative Vice Lords Launch Improvement Drive

The Conservative Vice Lords have launched a two prong program to improve their neighborhoods by helping tenants fight slum landlords and by conducting a major clean up drive.

The C.V.L. Inc. has received $25,000 from the Field Foundation, plus 100 Neighborhood Youth Corps positions from the Catholic School Board to administer a summer program of beautification.

"Where there was glass, there will be grass," Spokesman Bobby Gore told a press conference.

"The need for this program is obvious to anyone who walks the streets of Lawndale. The curbs are lined with filth, papers fly in the face of passerby, and parkways are covered with glass."

Glenn Smith of CVL is director of the program. Neighborhood youth will sweep streets, paint trees, and plant grass and flowers.

"We have already seen the enthusiasm our program generated in the community," Gore added.

WHERE THERE WAS GLASS THERE WILL BE GRASS

Bobby Gore, president of the Conservative Vice Lords, Inc., described his group's $25,000 beautification project to newsmen at a press conference last week. Crews of young men will be employed to plant grass and keep the neighborhood clean.

Conservative Vice Lords, Inc. member, Percy Williams, describes the new Tenants Rights Action group he heads. The group will try to stop slumlords from using illegal means to evict people.

"Neighbors volunteer to help; a block club donated grass seed; an eighty year old man wanted to know how he could help and kids and adults both water grass in the evening."

The CVL members extended their thanks to the Field Foundation, the Catholic school board, Alderman Collins and Mayor Daley for providing the equipment.

"The cooperation and coordination of these several groups with CVL Inc. with no strings is an example of the kind of support we need," Gore said.

The second prong of their program is directed against slum landlords "who prey on tenants and threaten them with eviction when the tenants become hip to the bad conditions of buildings."

They have organized a Tenants Rights Action Group directed by Percy Williams. "We will block illegal evictions—legally if we can, forcefully if we must. We fight for tenant rights as hard as we used to fight among ourselves," they added.

The CVL has already stopped four illegal evictions this week.

'West Side Story' is an outdated tale; '80s gangs more violent, sophisticated

Gang Peace Raises Hopes

AN EDITORIAL

Chicago's civil-rights movement has, for a number of years, been the target of ridicule because of the unorthodox way it has tried to eliminate some of the basic inequities in the ghetto and as a result of the movement's failure to direct attention to a positive unification program.

What has happened, basically, is that the movement has blundered along aimlessly, realizing few victories; and every constructive effort made to develop a solid foundation has been stymied by a disgruntled hierachy that has created more divisions than unity.

It's saddening to konw that Chi "black men of prominence" have not yet ed the value of cohesion.

What is encouraging, though, is tha youths, who have been forced to ke their own way in a society that ills by promoting paternalism willing to travel the

Chicago Gangs Aid In City Violence Control Efforts

Two Gangs Set Up Centers For Helping Riot Victims

Street Gangs Set New Tone for Chicago

BY D. J. R. BRUCKNER
Times Staff Writer

CHICAGO — The Conservative Vice Lords are becoming so successful at operating businesses in the city's west side ghetto that they are seeking professional education in management techniques just to keep up with their own progress.

The CVL, a federation of 26 neighborhood gangs, with more than 8,000 members, owns and operates a malt shop known as Teen Town, two pool halls, an agency which provides security guards for a Negro-owned construction company, an employment referral service run in connection with the Urban League, an art gallery which is also an art school, a tenants union and a crafts shop.

They also run summer programs, such as street cleaning and neighborhood beautification drives which they sponsor and police, bus ride outings for neighborhood children and sandlot ball leagues. They are setting up a newspaper distributorship for the area, where newsboys' fear of being on the streets has virtually eliminated home distribution for many years.

They have two teen-age "hang-ins" called Houses of Lords), small meeting places with ping pong tables and other amusement equipment for youths. They hope to have at least one of these associated with each of their 26 organizations. Beyond that, they hope that each of the 26 affiliates will be opening businesses—laundries, car repair shops, gasoline stations, restaurants.

Reign of Terror

They have come a long way from the rumbles, the intergang warfare and what amounted to a reign of terror only a few years ago when the Vice Lords were more notorious, more feared and more pursued by the authorities than even the famous Blackstone Rangers on the south side.

The leaders of that old-time warfare are now the leaders of the CVL organizations. They call themselves old-timers sometimes; a few of them are even over 30. Their memories of the gang warfare run back into the 1950s. Their decision to do something different dates to around 1964 or 1965 when they decided they were headed down a blind alley.

Early last year they obtained a charter from Illinois, and they are now known as the Conservative Vice Lords, Inc. They are a nonprofit corporation which plows some earnings back into its businesses and uses the rest to open new businesses. A seven-man board of directors decides on all new projects, allocates funds and keeps a fantastic range of contacts in government and business.

Starting to Pay

They started their malt shop partly on a grant from the Rockefeller Foundation and with matching funds from a local group, and they have received some other assistance; but their businesses have begun to generate their own income.

Now they are preparing to use another grant to bring some managerial experts into their projects to give advice, but not to make decisions, and to train their own leadership in sophisticated management. Robert Gore, the spokesman (spokesman is a title, not a description) for the CVL board of directors, says, "We have found we are getting just a little bit beyond our knowledge of how the world really works. There are a lot of things, technical things, you have to know in business and that is what we are seeking now."

Gore says they incorporated for several reasons. It gave them the look of respectability they were seeking. But, much more important, it gave them a definite structure, which few street gangs achieve, and legal rules under which they must operate. In a sense, he says, the articles of incorporation were devised for self-discipline and training.

Some Lawndale youths poke a little fun at the CVL. One youth watching a reporter leave the CVL headquarters recently, said jeeringly, "Those guys even get along with the cops."

Meetings With Police

They do, after a fashion. They have initiated many meetings with police commanders on neighborhood problems, and even had one police commander sit in on some of the meetings at which they decided to incorporate themselves.

There are still a few incidents, but the CVL

W. Clement Stone

Endorse's **Vice Lords**

Vice Lords Art Show Traces Black History

Ghetto Fashion Spa Has Roaring Start

By Abra Anderson

The African Lion opened Wednesday with a roar of miniskirts, steak bone jewelry and hopes for a productive future in the black community.

A jazzy boutique American style is the Lord

and necklaces of steak bone, wire and wood, designed by Herbert Wilkinson, another Chicagoan, start at for a set.
Bobby Gore,

Chicago was depicted in the ntings.
evident thruout much of the abit was the theme of civil hts, balanced by black pride. he Lords are a west side eet gang. They opened the tery last September, and er classes in various art, nnique, Ralph Arnold, pro-nent black artist, was the lery's artist-in-residence for ew weeks.

Vietnam hero

City medal given former gang chief

What lies ahead for gang members who go straight?

'Art And Soul' Tries To Bring Black Culture

By THURMAN KELLEY

Art and Soul was designed by local artists and the Conservative Vice Lords, Inc. to bring to Lawndale a Black Culture which is sorely needed. Black Culture is still in the Black woman's womb. She needs to be educated to the awakening of it. Black culture has a broad base dealing with music, literature, paintings, soul food and our daily activities.

It has been suppressed; but now it is an embryo; it has a chance to live and love without being denied the knowledge of one's true self. The Black child started to appreciate being called a Black Nigger. Without being upset while being called out of your name. Now that our emotions have become changed to our benefit instead of our downfall.

We have seen this year, great numbers of Black Artists and related fields on television as decrease in size. Only the people who pay the dues achieve their success. So, Art and Soul will have a task of bringing the Black community into the mainstream of Americanism.

With the chance of Black children knowing what they want out of life, and to be willing to pay the price. But not through the nose. Since our 'Black children's talents have been wasted, now is the time to change its directions. Our youth is our product, their tie is our success.

Black culture is our vehicle—if we do our thing, we will achieve our success. Art and soul will use its full resources on Black culture to the fullest extent of completing one's individual self. With the help of Black artists they will instruct workshop classes and give in-

Brother Larry Bailey does his thing at Art and Soul.

formation in lectures on their own particular fields of art with classes on Tuesday, Wednesday, Friday and Saturday.

Art and Soul is here by definition: to make Black Students their prime concern is how to relate to the brothers in the streets. The process of analyzing the question occurs within an academic and social structure erected on the white American experience. So therefore, in such an environment, the Black student for his evolving Black consciousness, acceptance, awareness, articulation, and development of the Black experience, to completing the framework for answering the question, C.V.L. has a vehicle to use talents of the Black students as well as Black community, a community project. The chance is ours. Let us make the best of it.

Brother Jackie Hetherington points out a painting at "Art and Soul".

"The Peace Corps: Making It In The Seventies,"
Joseph H. Blatchford

It is common for Americans to ask today, "Why go overseas when there is so much to be done at home?"

The answer to the question is also best exemplified in the nearly 40,000 Volunteers who have now served in the Peace Corps and returned home.

After living among the poor abroad and struggling in the agonizing process of change, they are not satisfied with "band-aid" cures.

It is not surprising that 40 percent of Volunteers change their career plans while in the Peace Corps or that upon returning they continue a life of service to society.

The young man in Chicago who helped transform a Chicago street gang into a thriving economic development corporation is one of the more dramatic examples of the hundreds who have begun a life of promoting social change.

Foreign Affairs, October, 1970

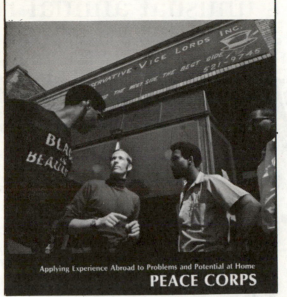

Applying Experience Abroad to Problems and Potential at Home

PEACE CORPS

Vice Lord

If the Great Originator is thinking of wiping out mankind and starting over, editorialized *Esquire* in a recent issue, there are some human beings who might cause him to change his mind. In the magazine's list of "Twenty-seven people worth saving" was DAVID G. DAWLEY '63.

At some point in his undergraduate career Dave reached the decision to sublimate the desire for personal gain and to work for his less fortunate neighbor, to give him the chance to progress economically and spiritually. As apprentice training for such a career he joined the Peace Corps, receiving field training at Taos, New Mexico, and a two-year assignment in rural Honduras. Through this experience he found out what it means to stand out in a crowd, and to be able to deal objectively in a strange, multi-colored environment. Later he received a master's degree in community organization from the School of Social Work at the University of Michigan.

In the summer of 1967 he was selected by the Association of the Trans-Century Corporation to participate in the evaluation of federally funded summer programs. He was sent to the Lawndale section of Chicago to interview residents in that seething ghetto. Lawndale, on Chicago's West Side, is an area of some twenty square blocks of rundown tenements, with many of the ugly features of the Harlem, Watts, and Washington ghettos.

Dawley quickly learned that the area was controlled by an 8,000-member organization known as the Conservative Vice Lords who, in the early '60s had been street fighters, stomping and mugging through Lawndale's avenues and alleys. Now, in 1969, the core of the Vice Lords consists of men in their early thirties, with perhaps two years of secondary education — dropouts and "throw-outs." This group had finally determined among themselves that riot and destruction were getting them nowhere, and had turned to a program of rebuilding. They were sorely in need of an organizer, coordinator, and developer. Dave Dawley proved to be a natural for the job.

CVL's unusual annual report

It's called "A Report to the Public." At first glance, you'd think it's the usu... report of a public ... agency. The forma... Plenty of picture...

pitching pennies and sipping wine," Gore recalls. "Then one of the young fellows said- he take about 50 others ...al attack

"would not believe that a street gang could overcome some of the problems that, as teen-agers, the gang members had caused

whether or not munity can operatively a ... with the youn...

African Lion

Until recently, there was very little awareness on the West Side of Chicago of the rich cultural heritage that other groups of Black Americans have felt. To encourage pride in black history and to expose black residents of the West Side to the rich heritage of Africa, Conservative Vice Lords Inc. created the African Lion— a soul shop that manufactures and sells original garments.

Through the African Lion, CVL intends to develop an identity with Africa as well as to sell black clothing. The development of an Afro-American identity for Black Americans should not be considered a separatist movement but rather a search by people for meaning.

Most of the ethnic groups that settled the United States have clung to the heritage of their ancestors. We believe that the development of respect for an African heritage will offer a sense of pride and dignity that will prepare black people to cope more adequately with the degradation, discrimination, and exploitation that are part of daily life in the ghetto.

The extent to which black people can cope with ghetto life an... fight to eradicate the sicknes... perpetuates ghetto condi... extent to which ou... will have the st... dreams we ...

West Side Development Corporation

West Side Community Development Corporation. As one of five groups in the West Side Community Development Corporation (WSCDC), CVL received a cash award at the first annual conference of the "Strategy For The New City" 1969-72, "for its emerging role in establishing a strong economic and political community in the 'New City.' The West Side Community Development Corporation was commended because represented in it are five organizations that have rejected old rivalries and banded together because they recognize the root of the community's problem as economic."

Management Training Institute

The Coalition for Youth Action of the U.S. Department of Labor has funded a Management Training Institute to prepare young Vice Lords for positions of responsibility within small business enterprises.

Twenty young brothers and sisters are enrolled in a twenty-week program that teaches black history, self aware-

ness, reading, and such diverse business skills as banking, accounting, business correspondence and salesmanship.

The Management Training Institute fulfills a critical need of many young fellows who hang out on the street or hustle to survive—fellows with high intelligence but low opportunity.

By giving youth an investment in the community and hope in the future, the CVL business ventures, neighborhood action and training begin to solve the crisis of development on the West Side.

A fight for life

"Like society itself, we are in a time of change. Just as we used to fight each other on the street, we now stand together in a different fight for life—the life of a city, the life of a neighborhood, and the life of people who have been declared unemployable, uneducable, and unreached." (Comment of Alfonso Alford, President of the Conservative Vice Lords, when the group became a not-for-profit corporation in the State of Illinois in September, 1967.)

In the past two years, the 8,000-10,000 Vice Lords in twenty-six segments on the West Side of Chicago have moved from streetfighting to business development and community improvement. This report analyzes that change, describes some of CVL's current programs, and notes our hopes for the future.

Sustaining a hope

Alfonso Alford has emphasized that while CVL has awakened youth to the dream of something new, society must sustain the hope that has been generated.

"We must continue to stimulate economic growth and social awareness, and by involving alienated youth in the life of a community, CVL Inc. performs a valuable service to the country.

"The Supreme Court and Congress have acted on the rights of people, but it is the actions of people that will determine how we survive. People cannot be told what to do; billyclubs will not earn respect for the law; nor will mace bring the diverging races together.

"By working together with friends, industry and government in the common task of improving life, CVL can do much to reverse the hopelessness, bitterness and misunderstanding among people."

The conditions in Lawndale have been described, analyzed, discussed and reported, yet the simple fact is that the conditions have remained unimproved. Housing has not been found, and education has not been improved. Many of the social ills of our community are too complex for us to prescribe a solution, but one of the problems we have done something about is the filth and litter that fill our streets.

In the summer of 1968, with 100 Neighborhood Youth Corps positions from the Catholic School Board and a grant from the Field Foundation of Illinois, CVL led a movement to beautify the community. CVL members swept streets, picked up trash and planted grass. Parkways that usually remain brown and littered became green and clean.

The National Advisory Council of Economic Opportunity recommended in "Focus on Community Action," a report to the President in 1968, that "continuing efforts be made to identify, reach, and serve the hard core poor in each community —in the full realization that such efforts will be more difficult, more costly, and disproportionately less visible in results."

Our program not only served but was conducted by the "hard core." This is an example of "Inreach," the CVL concept to involve youth that society has rejected. We do not have to reach out, as many institutions must. We simply have to reach in because we are them. We do not have to expend valuable time gaining rapport with the street corner society because we have been brothers of the street since we were born.

Making the west side the best side

ELDRIDGE CLEAVER

A chance to make it

As a gang CVL ruled the streets of Lawndale. Cars were stocked with shotguns, young men were mauled in street battles and many were arrested and sent to jail.

Today, although some of us are still restless, most want a chance to make it without fighting, stealing, or throwing molotov cocktails. We began to turn "conservative" one hot night in July, 1964. Bobby Gore, who is now the spokesman for CVL, remembers that leaders from about 8 of our 26 groups were together in one of the usual hangouts.

We were sitting around pitching pennies and sipping wine. Then one of the younger fellows said he wanted to take about 50 others on a fall. We asked him why and who he wanted fall on—had anyone misused him? His reply was that the older lords had made a name and they wanted to keep it alive. We sat up all night. We told them how we saw people begging not to be hit any more with a baseball bat or chain how guys got cut up, how the people and how police would hate their guts and how he might be the one who got killed.

Finally, one of the younger fellows said, well, we have to do something. We can't get jobs, we're too old to go back to school, we're too big to play games. What else is there to do?

There was something else to do and CVL Inc provided the answer. CVL decided to try to change the conditions that make a man get a gun and hold up a store that make him drink scrap iron to forget about the lousy conditions in which he lives, that lead a guy to hustle dope and to have the family he wants to support but cannot.

The most common feeling on the West Side of Chicago has been one deeply felt by most black people the

feeling of hopelessness. In a state that receives a multi-million-dollar atom smasher a young Vice Lord cannot afford a decent haircut before going out for a job interview in a city so rich that it can rebuild McCormick Place West Side mothers cannot find a place to have their children while they look for a job.

CVL has vowed to see that our community and children get the chance to make the West Side the Best Side. There was tremendous skepticism now ever. The public would not believe that a street gang could overcome some of the problems that, as teenagers, the gang members had caused.

But CVL would not accept the young whose future was clouded with a brutal legacy. We could not turn our backs on them. Bobby Gore said we were and are the last resort for many and if we didn't listen who would?

The programs and enterprises that CVL has developed since September 1967 are examples of how a group with effective leadership and strong social responsibility can transform destructive energy into constructive progress if given appropriate and adequate financial and technical assistance.

CVL programs demonstrate the pride that black people must feel to free themselves from the fatalistic feeling that nothing can be done the resignation that life cannot be changed the despair that nobody cares and the belief that snatching purses and drinking scrap iron is the only way to make it.

CVL has awakened fellows on the street to the dream of something new. If we are to sustain the hope that CVL has generated then we must continue to build pride along with economic growth and social awareness.

From a vague dream

David Dawley, Consultant to CVL, describes the progress of the Vice Lords as developing from a "group of men with a vague dream into an active corporation conducting diverse programs, establishing CVL as a unique contribution to the constructive development of our urban areas.

"In a time when society is searching for answers to the chaos and violence which are infusing our national life; in a time when unemployed black teenagers feel no hope, a youth group in the ghetto has provided us with the opportunity to do something about the problems of our cities. A unique aspect of the Conservative Vice Lords is that youth on the streets have proposed the course of action; solutions were neither suggested nor imposed by outside people. The opportunity was not developed by white society, but by black youth."

Teen Town

Once a gutted storefront, Teen Town is now a first-class ice cream parlor with wall panelling and sparkling equipment. The corner at Sixteenth and Lawndale—center of an area that the Chicago *Sun Times* described as having "more problems for a square block than any other in the city"—is now a symbol for what youth on the West Side can achieve.

Different Strokes for Different Folks

People can walk around Sixteenth Street now with watches and rings on, and women with pocketbooks don't have to worry about us bothering them. If anybody does bother them, most of them come to the CVL office and find out if somebody can help them. Every time there's a problem around here, the people come to us. We don't threaten them or command them; it's something they want to do.

The hierarchy was seeing some of the good we were doing, but they still labeled us a gang and didn't give us time to deal with the problem. They know they have misused people and they saw us taking votes away from them.

In May 1969, Mayor Daley had a press conference and announced his war on gangs. He said, "Throughout the country, there has been a glorification of this gang structure and that's why it's so serious today." He said gangs are vicious and got us back in that stereotype bag. These guys are making decisions about all groups just by what some groups or some individuals do. They give the impression that everybody is the same and nobody can change.

Mayor Daley gets most of the votes from his patronage system in the ghetto. He has a handpicked administration behind him, and if you don't dance to his music, you lose your job. They do almost nothing for black folks. Garbage collection once a month, plenty of liquor stores, free chickens, a half pint of whiskey or a couple of bucks at voting time. All we gotta do is sit back and be cool: don't say nothin', follow procedures; you're gonna walk the milky white way and everything gonna be peaches and cream, milk and honey. Just stay down here and do what the white folks say do and when you die you get your reward if you be good niggers. This is the philosophy they dropped on our people.

But to Bobby, Mayor Daley is "just another cat off the street. He's not like this cat Lindsay in New York. When they have problems in

New York, Lindsay would come out of that office, man, and go out in the street and mingle with the people and try to find out what the real problem was. Mayor Daley, he don't really care. His thing is to keep his chest out and to deal only with politics. He plays his tune simply by what he hears from reports. And from some of the things this cat say on TV, his administration is not clickin', like it should.''

The Mayor should talk about himself when he talks about glorifying gangs because he is Chicago's most glorified gangbanger. In August 1969 in the Chicago *Journalism Review*, Henry De Zutter wrote that Mayor Daley ''is a former president of the Hamburgers, who started as a tough bunch of streetfighters. It was in 1919 — when Daley was 17 — that the famous race riot exploded on the south side. Some of the bloodiest attacks on Negroes by whites occurred right in the middle of the Mayor's neighborhood. The record notes that white gangs were the chief assailants.''

The *Journalism Review* quotes the riot commission study which said that ''Gangs and their activities were an important factor throughout the riot. But for them, it is doubtful if the riot would have gone beyond the first clash. Gangs whose activities figured prominently in the riot were white gangs or athletic clubs. The stockyards district (Daley's neighborhood) is the home of many of these white gangs and clubs.''

The riot commission also said, ''Responsibility for many attacks was definitely placed by many witnesses upon the 'athletic clubs' including Ragen's Colts, the Hamburgers, Aylwards, Our Flag, Standard, . . . and several others. The mobs were made up for the most part of boys between 15 and 22.

''Gangs particularly of young whites, formed definite nuclei for crowd and mob formation. Athletic clubs supplied the leaders of many gangs.''

Mayor Daley doesn't say much about these years when he was a kid. Maybe he's still fighting the race riot of 1919.

Even so, Captain Buckney, when he was chief of the Gang Intelligence Unit, probably was not referring to the Mayor when he said that gang leaders ''are hard-core criminals. They are not redeemable, and anybody who thinks they are is wasting his time.''

Some of Captain Buckney's strategy for the war on gangs was revealed in *Chicago Today* on June 5, 1969, when he was quoted as saying that some of his men occupy themselves ''keeping things stirred no'' between the gangs.

An example of this is when Bobby heard that information was passed to the Blackstone Rangers and the Disciples that if any of them came to the West Side, we would kill them. Automatically this is going to provoke hard feelings. But we were able to stop any trouble by contacting the Rangers and Disciples to tell them this was just a rumor.

Another thing the police have done is pick up one gang member and drop him off in an enemy neighborhood. They have done this to the Blackstone Rangers and Disciples in the last few years, and they used to do this to the Vice Lords and Egyptian Cobras.

The police would come out here and catch a Vice Lord and drop him off in a Cobra neighborhood. They would make it known that he is a Vice Lord and let him worry about getting himself out. They might say, "He told me about how many of you guys he did this to and how many guys he did that to, and well, we just thought that maybe you could talk to him."

They leave you right there. If you can manage to get to a phone, you could call the police a thousand and one times and have no response. So you try and run, get out of there the best way you can. In the old days you'd get a pretty good whipping; you'd get hit in the head with a baseball bat or chain. But now there's a lot of shooting involved and when you get dropped off in a neighborhood like that, you don't have nothin' less than a killing comin'.

When the police say, "I got a couple of Cobras over in the car and they say they shot a couple young dudes and the Vice Lords ain't crap," the young cats will take this to heart and right away they want to do something without checking.

Some of the guys have heard us and we have to motivate them into positive thinking so they will slip out of a crowd like that and make sure one of us knows what's going on.

In one instance, Calloway happened to be on the set and saw what was going on. He told the police, "Well, yeah, we gonna handle that." The police left grinning. Calloway asked the little brothers if they had any carfare. He said now see what they're doing? They're trying to get these little brothers in a jam. We gave them carfare to go on home and we stayed there with them until they caught the bus to leave.

We're supposed to be the criminals, but what kind of police department does a thing like this?

We were probably the only ones who listened to the Kerner Commission report. We didn't need a report to know what was happening, but in 1968 to reduce tension and work toward understanding, we held an open house for police. We sent personal letters inviting Daley, Hanrahan, Buckney, the district commanders, detectives, and patrolmen:

> There have been many misunderstandings between police and the community. As a group once identified with gang activity, we have had confrontations with the police which at times we caused but which at other times were provoked by the police.
>
> Many police cars cruise through our neighborhood and peer into the windows of our programs. Perhaps these policemen do not feel they would be welcome if they simply came in to see what was happening.
>
> Therefore, in the hope of changing attitudes and developing understanding on the street, we are inviting the police department to visit our programs.

We reserved one day for policemen only. We had free coffee and doughnuts, and Lords guided policemen through the programs. Some police from the districts came and there was an understanding developed by both sides. But Buckney and Hanrahan did not come. They were willing to declare war on us, but they would not even come out to see what we were doing.

Our best communication with the police was with the district police, not with downtown. In developing programs our first move was to talk with Commanders McCann and Simms of Marquette and Fillmore so they would understand what we were trying to do. But the downtown brass makes all the policy and most of the patrolmen are not in touch. The patrolmen are not told that this is a group that's trying to do something. They remember Vice Lords with capes and chains and this is who they are out to get.

Some officers have come around and spent time with us to find out our problems. But the hierarchy hears about this and they ice it. The officers don't come around any more so there's no communication.

Shortly after the Mayor announced his war on gangs, Commander Simms was ordered by the Police Department to get out of Bootstrap. He had been a founder of Bootstrap, acting chairman for months, and one of the most active members. Now he was forced to leave because the city was trying to isolate gangs for the extermination they planned.

Commander Simms was even ordered not to talk with gang leaders. In 1967 his talking with the Lords prevented a riot from starting after a white cop shot a black youth. In 1969 the Police Department created more tension by cutting off all communication. They wanted to provoke us into shooting so they could come in and crush us. But if they want extermination they're going to be exterminating for a long time. The minute they eliminate us they're gonna have some more come up.

We went into Bootstrap and told them there had not been a gang clash on the West Side in a few years. We said we had come to Bootstrap to get some expertise from the businessmen. As Bobby says, "I'm a high school dropout and don't know nothin' about runnin' no restaurant, but we're willing to try."

The restaurant had been open for more than a year and Bobby told them that "now the system is gonna put their thumbs down on everything that is called black youth. When people pick up the paper and read about what one gang did and another gang did, they say all are in the same category. But this is not so."

The businessmen knew why Commander Simms left Bootstrap and we knew. We wanted some action and dropped some questions on Bootstrap that they never did answer. We told them that they were willing to take credit for some of our programs and asked where they were when forces are needed to defend justice, not just law and order? We asked why people are destroying the good when trying to control the bad? We asked if Bootstrap would accept repression like the McCarthy era or would they stand up for justice? We asked why they didn't speak, why they let this happen?

After Bobby got through talking, all the chairman could say was that this would have to come under "new business." They had to follow procedures and agendas and refused to deal with the issue so we just walked out.

Bootstrap had the chance to do something, but those cats from Sears Roebuck, Western Electric, Ryerson Steel, Illinois Bell and the Urban League just sat there playing with themselves.

Commander Simms had been involved in an effective police community relations program and was iced, and Bootstrap would not stand up to say anything. Daley and Hanrahan were talking about extermination and these cats had to go by the agenda.

There had been good that came out of Bootstrap, but for more than a year we had been telling them that they were going the wrong route. In July 1968 we delivered a paper to Bootstrap that reviewed our experiences during the previous year and described changes which would make Bootstrap acceptable.

We reminded them that we attended meetings, listened to reports and waited for action during the year since Bootstrap was formed. We were asked to prepare reports for monthly meetings, and we prepared reports. We were asked to write down what we needed, and we wrote down what we needed. We were patient.

But although Bootstrap matched the Rockefeller grant, they were not listening. After a meeting in the Sheraton Blackstone Hotel on April 16, 1968, when we helped them raise money, Bootstrap suddenly stopped having monthly meetings. The letterhead stationery was printed with the address of the YMCA and an acting director was appointed despite the objection of the street groups. This director was also deputy director of Youth Action, the social agency street work program, and we wanted Bootstrap created so we could move away from that bag.

Bootstrap was supposed to help us find the owners of vacant lots, but nothing happened. Christmas gifts were distributed to families on the West Side from Operation Bootstrap, Youth Action and the Sears YMCA. There was no mention of the clubs but we were the ones giving out the gifts. Newspaper stories gave credit to Bootstrap for opening programs that they didn't open.

We wrote our criticisms to the executive committee of Bootstrap on May 8, 1968, but the committee did not even answer our letter. In July we wrote that by working with agencies, we hoped we could improve our clubs, but this partnership had failed.

"We have come too far on our own to see our efforts delayed by unproductive meetings and waylaid by misleading publicity. We find ourselves now in a familiar bag: where Bootstrap was conceived as an effort to support what the clubs are doing, Bootstrap is now absorbing clubs into programs that Bootstrap is creating. Rather than helping the clubs to develop, Bootstrap is competing with the clubs. The original intention of Bootstrap has been lost; there is too much structure and there is too much mutual distrust."

We proposed three changes:

1. Remove all social agencies.
2. Change the name of Operation Bootstrap to reflect a coalition between industry and the clubs.
3. Agree to redefinition of the concept of this coalition and reorgani- zation of the structure.

These requests were rejected and not a single businessman voted with us. Even the Cobras and Saints voted to keep the social agencies, though after another year they felt we had been right. By then Bootstrap was dead, and even the businessmen were kicking dirt on the grave. We had told them to back up, but they didn't hear anything we were saying, or didn't want to hear because if they really did anything, the Mayor might be upset and call up the chairmen of these companies. Then somebody would get fired. So instead of dealing with the truth, these guys are steady pretending to help.

Bootstrap was not the only group that would not stand up to the machine. Since the war on gangs in 1969 and scandals about extortion on the South Side in 1970, the newspapers have wanted only the blood and guts stories. The Chicago *Sun-Times* and Chicago *Daily News* have told the story of CVL programs, but since the war on gangs, all newspapers and television stations have failed to tell how CVL has developed new programs. They ask when was the last Vice Lord killing or how many times was somebody stabbed or shot, not how is the restaurant going.

The Fillmore Police District is a Vice Lord district and in 1968 the *Daily Defender* asked, "Why does Englewood (South Side, Chicago) become a 16-man coffin while Fillmore's death arrest rate for juveniles drops 66 per cent?" But the downtown newspapers didn't write a story about how in 1969 the overall crime rate in the city went **up** 7.2 per cent and crime went down in only two police districts, one of which was Marquette, where we have most of the CVL Inc. programs, and that went **down** 4.4 per cent. Nobody asked why the crime rate was down in Marquette when that district used to be among the highest crime districts in the city.

To the city every shooting is a gang shooting and this gives them high statistics and an excuse for coming in with shotguns like they did on Black Panthers Fred Hampton and Mark Clark. But you can't fault the whole community for something an individual does and you can't fault every group for something one group does. Years ago, black people didn't even get time for killing each other. Now since the young people are getting together, all of a sudden all the killings are gang killings.

They also talk about extortion and give the impression that this goes on throughout the city. But who talks to the businessmen along Sixteenth Street? We used to terrorize this street, but now some of the businessmen advise us on what we're doing. When some fellas from another group came through and tried to extort these businessmen, one of the younger Lords declared that he wasn't going to let them come around and do that.

"I got some stock involved in Lawndale and I got too much pride to let somebody come around and fuck up what I helped put together.

People who said they were Lords have sometimes tried to extort, but when we find out this is going on, we put a stop to the shake down. In 1969, Commander Simms let us know that a cat was going around saying he was Bobby Gore and wanted money. The Commander found out this was some guy who was using a business card with Bobby's name on it.

Furthermore, when people talk about extortion they should talk not just about what some young people may be doing but about the police also. These guys are on the take and many nights you see those white shirts and gold braids go in the taverns.

Why listen to a system that says you're extorting when you're not and closes its eyes when the police are out here shaking down and taking bribes?

All we asked was for a chance to show what we were talking about. We're not going to turn eight to ten thousand Vice Lords into Boy Scouts overnight and we're not going to get every guy, but what do you have left if a war on gangs crushes everything that CVL has started?

We're not a hoodlum gang any more and we don't approve of what some of these young cats are doing even though they may be Vice Lords. But society made us the bottom of the barrel, and after us there's no place to go but the graveyard or the penitentiary. If we don't stay in touch with all these cats, who is going to get to them? Who is going to talk to them if we can't?

Bobby wished those people standing back ridiculing us would try to deal with the cats we're dealing with, "'cause we got what nobody else wants. This shit don't just jump up here and if any of these cats thinks this is easy, he could try himself. We need time to deal with the problem and we need help."

The way things are now, people are so busy trying to hold a guy down that they don't give him resources to work with, so he just gives up and you're right back where you started. We still have some time to get this thing up off the ground, but we've got to get enough money down here to deal with the over-all problem.

We need outside help and we welcome anybody that's sincere in helping us. The foundations gave us money with no strings attached, but many people have been afraid to talk with us. They thought we couldn't work with businessmen or that we wanted to shoot honkies on sight. But we made many understand that we look at people for what they are. If a person is for real, then we can get along, and now is the time for the people that are real to get moving. We need people who will stick when the going gets rough and people who are honest in why they are getting involved and what they can do.

There have been several individuals who pulled some strings and took chances by helping CVL. Bernie Rogers, an insurance executive with Marsh & McClennan Inc., a descendant of Jane Addams, and a jet set swinger, was one of the first whites who wanted to help. When Dave brought him in we were just getting into Teen Town, and we had him in a corner for two hours to find out why he wanted to help. His contacts led to the development of Art & Soul and a close friendship between CVL and Sammy Davis Jr. When others began to back away from CVL when the war on gangs got hot, Bernie was still helping.

Frank Monahan risked his job by giving us what the local poverty program would not give us. Monahan is a young Chicago Irish Catholic who had been a Peace Corps Volunteer and was director of the Neighborhood Youth Corps program for the Catholic School Board. In the summer of 1968 he delegated one hundred federal Neighborhood Youth Corps positions to CVL. Until we had a press conference to announce that the program had started, the Mayor didn't know that we had federal money. By that time we were on the streets with brooms that Alderman Collins had hustled from the city. We were working and there was no scandal.

Morris Leibman, a partner of Leibman, Williams, Bennett, Baird & Minow and chairman of the National Advisory Council on Economic Opportunity, began helping CVL with legal issues in the fall of 1967 and was always available for personal consultation. The people along LaSalle Street, the Wall Street of Chicago, always watched suspiciously when one white boy and five of us in dashikis or overalls walked through the financial "canyon." The first time we walked into Morrie's office, some of the young lawyers probably wanted to call the police, but eventually many lawyers in the firm helped us with contracts and leases.

Meanwhile, Mike Coffield and Pat Murphy volunteered to help individual Vice Lords who needed lawyers for personal problems, providing representation that none of us could afford.

The Field Foundation of Illinois also took some risks when other organizations were just talking about reaching the hard core. They gave us money for the beautification program and the African Lion, and this was because Hermon Dunlop Smith, the chairman, and Robert MacRae, the staff consultant, saw that we were sincere in what we were trying to do.

Although Bootstrap was a group of businessmen we had problems working with, we did have close connections with others such as Time, Inc. The chairman of Time, Andrew Heiskell, got turned on to CVL at a meeting of Urban America in Detroit. Goat had run down what CVL was trying to do so Heiskell used his company to help. Charley Bear and Vivi Stiles in New York and Ken Dougan and Terry Murphy in Chicago helped negotiate a grant with the Ford Foundation and underwrote the costs of an annual report.

We need the government to do the same thing that these people have done, but what the government usually does is like the story Goat tells about the pony soldier:

"The pony soldier told the Indian chief all he wanted to do was build a fort wherever he wanted a fort built. And once the fort was built, the homesteader came. The Indian had to go along with the homesteader because the fort was giving him resources. And this was the string that came along with the fort. The fort was a form of infiltration.

"Once you are infiltrated by the government, by his strings, you become weak, a puppet. We're trying to give government the answer if they would stop being so damn bullheaded. Nations are dying, just like the poor Indian, for lack of resources. What do we tell eight to ten thousand Vice Lords when the program falls and they tried to do right? How do you tell 'em we got to be good when they been good. Where does the group go?"

We've been in this long enough to know that the city government really doesn't give a shit. We have guys that come and see our problems and want to help but then they go back and have to talk to the big man. Chicago got something like 7 million dollars for West Side renewal, but the money wasn't felt down where we are. Nobody even knew the money was in the neighborhood. Whereas with just thirty thousand dollars, CVL created changes that could be seen with the naked eye.

Bobby points out that "there were supposed to be programs for youth, but there weren't very many. The Urban Progress Center in Lawndale — that's the local poverty program — had an office four stories high, and there's nothin' but foxy young ladies in there. . . looks more like a fashion show or modeling school than something that's going to be meaningful to the community."

When we first began we did not want to depend on the government or the economic survival of the Vice Lords. But even after we did decide to get some government money, we couldn't because Mayor Daley had complete control over how every federal dollar in the city was spent. The only program which went around Daley was The Woodlawn Organization program to work with the Blackstone Rangers on the South Side and this ended up with a congressional investigation by Senator McClellan, and the Rangers were made out to be the worse cats in the world. As Goat says, "I ain't got time to be talkin' to a congressman from Arkansas."

There were people in Washington, like in VISTA, who wanted us to run a program, but they couldn't move because the mayor had Chicago uptight. The only government money we got other than the indirect program through the Catholic School Board came through the Coalition for Youth Action in the Department of Labor. These were college interns who had been given some money to give away so they wouldn't cause too much trouble inside the government.

The Coalition gave $32,000 to Youth Organizations United and this helped us sponsor the first Y.O.U. conference in East St. Louis, and they gave CVL a grant to open the management-training institute.

The establishment wouldn't drop a dime; the only federal money we got was from young white kids. In 1968 after agreeing to give Y.O.U. a grant of $750,000, Joe Califano in the White House; Willard Wirtz, Secretary of Labor; Wilbur Cohen, Secretary of HEW; and Bert Harding, acting director of OEO, suddenly backed off and the grant was not approved. McClellan coincidentally, was working over the Blackstone Rangers and The Woodlawn Organization. After the cities burned and everybody was talking about reaching the hard core, the government closed the door on the only national organization of hard-core youth.

We're trying to save not just black people but people, and even though we got all these programs and we're working with cats that nobody else will talk to, some of these guys from the outside don't even have time to come up from behind those desks or get out of those fancy Cadillacs to see what's going on. We invited Senator Percy to visit but on his next trip to Chicago, he went to see the Picasso statue in front of City Hall. He didn't have time for real people.

Daley, Hanrahan and Buckney have classified us as the worst people, but none of them came to our open house. Hanrahan was out here on Election Day in 1968* and came into Teen Town with a big smile and said what a wonderful job we were doing. He asked to have his picture taken with Bobby and then offered to do whatever he could when he got in office.

He kept his word; he did what he could to put everybody in jail.

On July 27, 1968, Alfonso was arrested and charged with murder. He was held without bail in the Cook County Jail and two months later, at 10 P.M., September 27, the jury found him not guilty. In his opening remarks to the jury, the prosecutor said, "We have no evidence" that Alfonso Afford killed this man; we are going to prove him guilty of murder on the theory of accountability. After Alfonso had spent two

---

* In November 1972, Edward Hanrahan failed to win reelection as State's Attorney for Cook County.

months in jail, the state admitted they had no evidence and the obvious intent to get the president of the Vice Lords was revealed. The state tried to prove that because Alfonso was president of the Vice Lords he was responsible for what happened on the street.

The jury heard witnesses say that a middle-aged man came out of his house firing a rifle. The man was drunk and had bumped into Alfonso on the sidewalk. The man's wife, who was sitting on a stoop, thought Alfonso had knocked him out of the way. She was also drunk and provoked her husband into getting his gun. When he came out firing, several people shot back at him across the street. One of these bullets killed him, and the State's Attorney tried to show that Alfonso was responsible.

The jury found Al not guilty, but for two months his number was 433986 in the Cook County Jail. And when everybody in the courtroom went home, there was still the lawyer to pay. The lawyer was the best in Chicago and the only string attached to his accepting the case was that CVL could not solicit money from the public. The lawyer thought this would reflect badly on his reputation; he didn't want to be accused of exploiting the poor. This case needed the best so Al accepted the condition.

But who pays for the cost of having to defend yourself? Who pays for the time away from your family? And who explains to the Ford Foundation that the president of the organization is in jail for murder?

These are the problems we faced in making the programs work. When Bobby says we were out there night and day, he means that to keep this shit together, we had to deal with these problems—the street and the man.

In February 1969 the pressures of street life caught up with Al. He had a stroke which temporarily paralyzed his right side and left him unable to speak. The club was slowed down without his leadership, and Bobby had to double up even more than before, running the office during the day and watching the street at night. Alfonso recovered slowly but even now he wears a leg brace, his right arm is weak, and his speech is limited. The fellas still look to him as the chief, but his condition prevents him from commanding the Nation with his old strength.

CONSERVATIVE VICE LORDS INC.

June 2, 1969

No Response

Mr. Edward Hanrahan
State's Attorney
2600 S. California
Chicago, Illinois

Dear Mr. Hanrahan:

Just as you are concerned with the violence on our streets which
is attributed to gangs, so are we interested in holding down the
shootings and disorders that are receiving widespread publicity
in the news media.

As you know, having visited Teen Town, we are a not-for-profit
corporation dedicated to self-help programs that develop social
and economic freedom for black youth in Chicago.

Since your visit to Teen Town, we have opened a clothing boutique, an
art studio, one Tastee Freez, two recreation centers, and a
"Management Training Institute." We have received support from
the Rockefeller, Ford, and Field Foundations as well as the U.S.
Department of Labor.

The street problems with which law enforcement groups must be concerned
jeopardize the success of these programs since the general public,
news media, and many public officials fail to distinguish between
constructive and destructive group activities.

We would be most interested in talking with you personally about
"gang" problems. Perhaps by talking with each other, we can develop
some ideas that will make the streets safe for everybody.

We would be glad to talk with you whenever and wherever convenient
but recognizing the seriousness of the issue, we feel this should be
as soon as possible. We would also be glad to show you our neighborhood
so that you can see first hand how far we have come.

Sincerely,

Kenneth Parks
Acting President

cc: Alderman George Collins
    Commander George Simms
    Commander William McCann

CVL INC. · 3720 WEST 16TH STREET · CHICAGO 60623 · (312) 521-9745

CONSERVATIVE VICE LORDS INC.

June 2, 1969

No Response

Mayor Richard J. Daley
City Hall
Chicago, Illinois

Dear Mayor Daley:

Newspapers and television have been filled with stories of gang violence. The Chicago public feels terrorized by the shootings on city streets, and the Chicago "Sun Times" has reported that you have conferred with State's Attorney Hanrahan, Police Superintendent Conlisk, and others to find new ways to cope with street-gang violence.

The Conservative Vice Lords are equally interested in reducing the violence on our streets. We are a not-for-profit corporation committed to the development of positive opportunity for our black brothers and sisters. Unlike many groups, we talk about what we have done rather than about what we intend to do. Our words are supported by action. We own and manage a restaurant, clothing boutique, Tastee Freez, pool room, and art studio, and we serve our community with programs in beautification, tenants rights, and youth training.

We have received program support from the Rockefeller, Ford, and Field Foundations, and we have managed a Neighborhood Youth Corps program and Department of Labor "Management Training Institute."

Street violence jeopardizes the programs we have developed. Consequently, we are concerned with reducing this violence as well as encouraging public officials, news media, and the general public to distinguish between constructive and destructive group activities.

We would like to talk with you to discuss our views on new ways to cope with street youth. We feel that our perpsective can contribute to your understanding of the problem and thus promote an effective plan to establish peace in our community.

We can meet with you whenever and wherever you wish. We feel that this meeting could benefit the entire Chicago community.

Sincerely,

Kenneth Parks
Acting President

cc: Alderman George Collins

Cell 103

Bobby became the street leader and by his recommendation Goat became acting president. Goat was responsible for the office and Bobby drew in tighter with Jesse Jackson, C. T. Vivien, and the West Side Community Development Corporation.

With the emergence of CVL as a powerful community organization and with Bobby in the leadership of the construction demonstrations, the State's Attorney targeted Bobby in his war on gangs.

About the time that Black Panthers Fred Hampton and Mark Clark were shot and killed by Hanrahan's raiders in a shoot-out, Bobby Gore was arrested for a killing on October 25,1969. According to several people, the eyewitness for the prosecution was an eyewitness only because he killed the man that Bobby was accused of murdering. But this guy was just another nigger and Hanrahan wanted Bobby because he was a leader.

During this time, Hanrahan also placed a charge of murder against Leonard Sengali, the spokesman for the Black P Stone Nation. But this time the prosecution's case was so weak that the judge had to instruct the jury to find the defendant not guilty.

Bobby was arrested on November 14, 1969, and five minutes after he was indicted a few days later, the State's Attorney's secretary was running to local newspapers with a statement that said the murder accusation against Gore "disproves the myth about the constructive activities of gangs and should cause foundations and others to intensify their scrutiny of persons seeking money from them to make certain those funds are not being used to arm street gangsters or for other idleness."

A man is supposed to be innocent until proved guilty, but Hanrahan announced his own opinion of the verdict before a jury was even selected.

A friend of Bobby's, Patrick Murphy, offered to help with the case until Bobby could find the lawyer of his choice. Murphy developed law programs as a Peace Corps Volunteer and had been Director of Urban Affairs for the National Legal Aid and Defender Association. Dave brought him in to defend Vice Lords in other cases, but Murphy accepted this one only to help prepare the case. The bond hearing was delayed several times by the state until finally Bobby was refused bail.

Before trial, while Bobby was in the Cook county Jail, Murphy interviewed witnesses who stated that Clarence Conn killed "Scab," the man Bobby was accused of killing. The State's Attorney's office talked with Murphy about this, even though some of these witnesses had testified before the Grand Jury that they had no knowledge of the killing. But this was before anybody was arrested and they were trying to protect Clarence Conn. When Conn fingered Bobby, Murphy tried to find new witnesses. When the case came up in the first week of January 1970 the defense moved for a continuance, and on January 26, when the case came up again, the defense moved for another continuance so that the lawyer Bobby wanted could enter the case. This lawyer had already been retained with cash. The court denied the motion and put the case over to January 28. On January 28 the defense was denied another motion and the case was set to January 29.

On January 28 the State's Attorney was notified that the defendant would request a trial continuance on January 29 because he was not ready for trial. Murphy told the court on January 29 that he was not prepared for trial, that he needed more time and that the state had furnished him a list of witnesses with phony addresses.

The lawyer Bobby wanted for trial, Eugene Pincham, also asked for a continuance so that he could appeal as co-counsel. He explained that he had recently been hired as co-counsel, that he had no knowledge of the facts, had not interviewed any of the witnesses, had not read any of the transcripts or prior proceedings and had not prepared the case for trial.

Bobby told the court he wanted to be represented by Pincham as well as Murphy and even though he was in jail he wanted a continuance so the lawyers could get prepared.

Judge Robert J. Downing denied the requests and called the trial for Monday, February 2, 1970.

Pincham told the Judge he could not prepare the case over a three-day weekend, and therefore Bobby would be denied effective counsel and counsel of his choice. Pincham told the Judge he would not appear in the trial.

When Bobby's request for a continuance was denied on January 29, there were 69 indictments pending for trial before the same judge. Bobby was charged in 2 of the 69 indictments for offenses that were committed on October 25, 1969. Including the two against Bobby, 5 of the 69 indictments occurred on October 25. Bobby's indictments were advanced for trial ahead of 62 previous indictments.

Of the 69 indictments, 52 were placed on trial call before Bobby's indictments were voted by the Grand Jury. Bobby's case was advanced for trial ahead of all these indictments.

Of these 52 pre-Bobby indictments, one murder indictment had been continued 51 times, another 49 times, another 33 times, two more 21 times each, and two more 11 and 13 times. None of the 52 had been continued less than 3 times, yet Bobby's indictments had been continued only 3 times—once by the state (December 8, 1969), once by the defendant (January 5, 1970), and once by the court (January 26, 1970).

Some of the 14 post-Bobby indictments had been continued 9 times and none had been continued less than twice.

On February 11, 1970, shortly after midnight, an all white jury found Bobby guilty. On March 10, 1970, he was sentenced to twenty-five to forty years in the state penitentiary in Joliet, Illinois.

From cell 103 at Joliet, Bobby wrote simply: "I didn't do this thing they accuse me of."

To Alderman Collins he wrote that he was "very much hurt at the way my trial turned out. I was not convicted on the evidence presented but for belonging to a so-called gang. I am sure the way things went that the State knew I didn't kill anybody. There were people who called the name of the guy who killed this youth. With what was presented during my trial against Clarence Conn, they had reason enough to at least investigate. They did not try me on the facts of the case which makes me certain it was a fix.

"It seems that all the labor CVL put into trying to help our black youth the best we could was in vain. I feel now that no one believed in us in the first place. Not one Bootstrap member showed up in court to even express concern. This also took me back a couple to years when Mr. Hanrahan and you were out to tour what we were doing. The man told us we were doing a fantastic job and to keep up the good work. We shook hands and grinned in each other's faces. And I see now it was just to promote his campaign and to fool our people.

"I'm not looking for any more than what my hand calls for. If I'm wrong, then I belong in prison. But if I'm not, then why should I be?

Is it to protect an image so Hanrahan can further his career? What about the thousands of kids out there who have no future, image, or career? What happens to them?"

In a letter to Dave, Bobby cried for his brothers: "If I had any idea that there was going to be a fight that night, I think I could have stopped it. Had I just stayed on the corner instead of going down the street, I would have been right there to stop it. Just the idea of those two black brothers losing their lives and the thought of how their families suffered is just about killing me.

"Brother, as you know, I had not gotten over losing my sister yet, which was the first time this kind of thing hit home for me, so my feelings must go with the families of those two dead kids. (Bobby's sister had died in the hospital after complications from a routine operation.)

"You know, Dave, it's odd that I be convicted of the very thing that I would have very gladly given my life to put a complete end to. But all my life things have been this way for me. I don't really know why, but I've always been one to worry about others, and each time I get to the place that I can help people, something always happens to cut my water off.

"But the hurting part is how these people sit back and say we misused the money we received without even coming out to see how it was being spent. Do they think those places jumped up by themselves? Don't they realize it took a lot of work by us? Don't they realize we didn't have any knowledge as to how this venture had to be handled? Instead of coming out and giving us help and knowledge, they stood back and made up stories about us stealing from ourselves.

"There is no other grass roots group that went as far as we did without expertise coming from anywhere. One thing that I can say and that's that I'm proud to have been part of it."

Bobby felt that CVL had taken the hopelessness out of most of the young cats, and in his letter to all the Lords he urged his brothers not to give up the fight.

"You cats can make the Lords' name ring in the history books as a group of gangbangers, as they call us, who were knocked to their knees by the system and wouldn't stay down but came back more powerful and determined than before to do your thing in the liberation of black people by refusing to stay down, to prove that given half a chance, you could do for yourself.

"Brothers, this is where you live. There's no place else to go that is not the same. So make what you already have a beautiful thing. If you succeed, then the system can't deny blacks nothing because what he calls the worst of humans proved him wrong. Never forget, WE ARE SOMEBODY!''

Keep the Love in the Club

One way or the other, we are going to have to stick together. Regardless of what names are used, blacks will be forced together and it's just a matter of waking up cats now so we don't waste thirty, forty, fifty years.

The future is uncertain and much of what happens will depend on how people react to what we're trying to do. We got some cats that are gangsters and we got some that are do-gooders. We got problems because we're dealing with what society has rejected, and they put this stereotype on us so that what one does, everybody does. People are not given a chance to show what's really on their mind.

They condemn the whole organization. But they didn't condemn the Congress when they found Bobby Baker wrong; they didn't condemn the Police Department when they found out that six policemen in the Fillmore District were members of the Ku Klux Klan; and they don't condemn the Boy Scouts when they catch them stealing cookies.

Bobby's pleas go unheard: "We're tryin', man, but they won't even give us a chance. We have shown some positive changes out here and this is not an easy thing. I got a twenty-four-hour job on my back and that's not only me. We got teenagers we take when we got to do our thing. We make sure that we have one of these cats with us so that he can learn what we're doing because there's no tellin' when we're gonna get rubbed out.

"To keep this thing going, we have to channel back down to the little brothers to give them a chance so they don't come up into this thing asleep and thinking all they gotta do is grow up and everything is alright. That's when trouble starts.

"If we're not successful we'll all go back where we came from. The entire country will get hurt. When a society is in a struggle and somebody slips back, everybody is gonna go back together. If you think the Panthers

177

are somethin', that will be just bullshit compared to violence in the street if cats become convinced that there is no goin' ahead.''

The attitude of some of the younger cats is that ''when you're a man you ain't supposed to suck dick.'' No man wants to die alone and the young cats say ''fuck that, I'm takin' everything I can with me.''

Like other people, the Lords have dreams. Some of these dreams may come true. In 1969, Cupid felt that in ten years ''we will have this whole thing. I might not be here to see it, but my kids will be here. I ain't gonna take half the shit my father took, and I don't want my kids to take none of the shit I took. I want to be able to run our own community. If we get this to rollin', we don't need that honky. I want our own black banks, our own black currency exchange—I don't want no honky to take my check and take forty or fifty cents: I want a brother to take it. I know when them honkies take it, its goin' back out to Oak Park or Lake Forest; it ain't doin' nothin' for the black community. I want to be able to go down to the Sheraton and just sign my name. Your name is money. You want to be able to walk in there same as anybody else and say here's my name, you take it.''

The neighborhood has begun to see changes in the club the way others see changes just in individuals. Toehold says ''the people in Lawndale don't feel like they felt five or six years ago. They was afraid of us and say we wasn't no good, just a bunch of gangbangers. But now some of them feel we right. They began to see what we're tryin' to do and a lot of them is helpin' us. Some have told us on the street what a wonderful thing we are doin' and how scared they was. They couldn't much walk the streets—guys would grab the ladies, pat 'em on the ass, squeeze their ass, call them a bunch of bitches. Now they can walk the street.''

Many a mother has come seeking help from the Vice Lords. The husband of one woman was deathly ill and three Lords went and donated blood. When somebody in the neighborhood dies, like Terry Collins, owner of the barbecue across the street from the pool room, we feel the loss. People got us pegged as something funny but we are real people.

People need something to grow on in the ghetto, and the philosophy of CVL is to take a man and motivate him so he can take care of himself. There are new ways of giving respect that streetfighting used to give. Instead of killing and destroying and tearing up, people can build if they get the chance. Goat says:

''I don't believe there's a man on this world that's completely dumb. I don't think God made a dumb man.''

One of the younger Lords admits that he was just "runnin' around doin' anything, didn't know what I was doin' 'til now," and Ting says that CVL "has treated me as if I'm a son and they are fathers or older brothers. And every business that we got, I done been in there and done some work. I have talked with people and did so much whereas I feel that this is my thing. I'm not gonna let nobody come in and fuck it up."

Goat says, "We're the old men that's gonna set up on the porches smokin' pipes and look back at what we started. We're gonna sit back and watch white and black folks laugh and talk and have fun and not say we must kill each other because he's black or white or he's dumb and not educated. Equal means a helluva lot more than just a few papers sayin' you got equal rights. You gotta have schoolin'. The same thing they teach in the suburbs must be teached here."

Even though CVL has had some grants and we have come as far as we have, there has also been a war declared on us, and the government by the people, for the people and of the people ain't done shit for us people.

White youth have also been misled and unless somebody wakes up, there will be just as much trouble from every kind of youth as there used to be just from us. Like Bobby Gore says, "The white college cats have listened to their parents; they got the money for college educations and different things and they are led to believe that we don't want anything for ourselves and that one rotten apple spoils the barrel. These parents tell their kids different stories they hear at work about the niggers. The kids listen to their parents and they are led to believe that we don't want to do anything to help ourselves.

"But you got a lot of kids out there that don't have to be out there doin' what they're doin' because their parents are filthy rich. But they want to use their own minds. They don't want to be brought up as a machine, or you're my kid, you're this, I'm gonna give you a Cadillac car — I'm gonna give you the best college education money can buy and all this shit and all I want you to do is help keep the black man down, keep the Puerto Rican down, or keep the Mexican down, the Indian down. They are teaching the kids to hate people they have never met. They hate so much some of them actually want to kill.

"The young white kids are rejecting this hate, and this has something to do with the formulation of the hippie thing. They listened to what their parents told them and found out that wasn't what was happening. Hippies treat you like people; they don't look at you and say, damn, you a whole lot darker than me.

"The rich white kids are just as bad off as a poor black kid because they are also getting hangups from the government. Some old cat from the suburban area is saying if you go over there, they'll kill you. But there are a number of whites who have been exposed and they find things aren't like the people have been telling them. They're finding out that people don't give a shit about them one way or the other. So they feel misused too."

Goat believes that "if you bring two dudes in here from the suburbs to meet ghetto people, a helluva shock would happen. Suburban people and ghetto people would find out one thing: that they are all people and that would be the biggest damn shock since Hiroshima because they don't know it now.

"If you're white and sit back and see that dude on TV, you say all them black folks dislike us. But if we were like people say, then Dave couldn't stay here. I don't guard Dave around.

"We have white groups that come in from suburban towns, bus loads of people, and we just take them on tours and explain to them what we are about, the past and the present. We don't get paid for this but certain things have to be done just to close the communications gap. There's some guys that come through that just need to know, and through these guys knowing, if they're sincere and get a feeling of what they see, then who knows who the next guy might talk to.

"CVL wouldn't have been what it is now if it wouldn't have been for a white guy* and I ain't pattin' him on the back. Before the white guy come in, there was no goal to build for. But when the white guy come in he said there is something you can do, and there was a goal. Now we build for that goal and we ain't gonna say the Puerto Rican and the Indian ain't fit to come up with us. Hell, we ain't no better than the people we goin' against 'cause all we doin' is creating another chain reaction against us in another ten to fifteen years.

"We got to have communication. Even before death there's communication. Before I kill you, I say I'm after you and you must die. There is communication. Now if you can communicate back, you might not die. But if you can't communicate back, you through, brother. So the ghetto kid and the suburban kid have got to learn to communicate."

Laughing is one form of communication and music is another. When you get a real good deep belly laugh, like Duke says, "One can come from China and one can come from Africa and they laugh in the same

*The white guy referred to is David Dawley. [Ed.]

language. There's no such thing as a Chinese laugh and a Japanese laugh and a Russian laugh or a black laugh or a white laugh.''

CVL has improved black/white communications through different programs. We had an old automobile agency building that we wanted to buy and we worked with Peter Gygax at the University of Illinois Circle Campus and got student architects to make designs for day care, movie making, recording studios, and classrooms. The building was just sitting there because businessmen were scared of vandals and we wanted a community center. We were not able to buy the building, but we did get the designs. Another group from the university taught photography to some of the fellas. These were all white students and we never had any trouble.

We're trying to end people being judged by what other people did. This is like us judging all white people by what other white people have done to us. But the way Goat feels, ''the people that created slavery is dead. How do I kill 'em again? Do I kill a guy that's white because his great great granddaddy put a colored man in the irons. My own great great granddaddy might have been an Uncle Tom that put a colored man in the irons. You gonna kill me? Am I gonna fight Dave Dawley from the Peace Corps? Hell, I'm twenty-six and he's twenty-seven and we fightin' over somethin' that happened back in the eighteenth century.

''We have to deal with the future, not the past. If we don't, there won't be no damn future because we will destroy the future with the past and everybody will lose. Unfortunately that's the direction we're going. We hope someone will see what's happening.

''The hippies are hippies because they went against the old structure that their parents had led and lived. If somebody doesn't do somethin', everybody gonna have his day — the hippie, the black, the Indian, the Mexican, the Puerto Rican. But if we're goin,' up the ladder, let's everybody go up. You dig?''

If they take us out of circulation, there will be more, and when they eliminate them there will be still more, and soon Daley, Hanrahan and Buckney will get what they are looking for. They will get a crowd that wants to destroy. A crowd that wants to destroy not property but people. All you need is some of these young cats who don't see both sides of the fence before making a decision, and the whole West Side is going to go amuck.

There are some young groups that are beginning to come up and they're at our back door. Our thing is to try to get to these cats and make some communications, but the way these cats ride us, it's going to come right back to where we were in 1961. These are young cats—thirteen, fourteen, fifteen—who want to establish reps and they see establishing reps as getting tough and shooting or fighting.

The Millard Boys, known also as the Black Aces, is one group that is coming out of the old turf bag, something Elzy grew up with but knows is an ancient idea.

''To get turf you went in there, kicked ass and showed the motherfuckers you weren't going to move. This went from fifty-four up until about sixty-three. We had identity, but we needed land to really establish our identity. We really didn't own the land but we thought this was ours. We paraded the streets and occupied certain corners. This was turf, man. But now, that's gone. We have started to think and see that this turf idea ain't shit. We saw this wasn't worth a fuck and wanted a change. So we started rappin'.

''The rap usually ended in fights, but then the raps stopped endin' in fights and more rappin' and more rappin' and we saw some stupid motherfuckers out there bashin' each other's heads. We say, 'Damn, Jack, it's some cold shit on the set today and nobody is doin' nothin' about it.''

''The Millard Boys can't grasp the idea of evolution. Behind like a motherfucker and can't grasp the idea of change. They want to revert. But we can't blame them too much because the situation here creates this shit. There's a lot of hard feelings because there have been shootings. But I try to dispel this feeling because these motherfuckers are my brothers. I don't want to do nothin' to them. This is a fact. But yet and still, I'm not gonna let them do nothin' to me. I wantta carry on and live too.''

We have to build, defend ourselves from the man and defend ourselves from these young groups coming up with violence. All this at the same time, and the white folks are steady looking for us to make everything peaceful overnight. White people have got to realize that the street doesn't always change as fast as some of the people do. Like in the wild West, sometimes they had to be tough to protect what they had built.

In one incident the Black Aces had been causing friction in the neighborhood and we went over to make a showing, like a march to let them know that we had numbers. The instructions were that nobody would bring weapons; we would just have a march.

Usually when you talk about going into another hood, the first order is to get your pieces. Whether you are going to fight or not, you have to have something to protect yourself with.

When we went over there we got fired on from out of the windows. Cars hit the brakes, made U-turns and all the fellas on foot ran.

"This was a march for peaceful coexistence with this little bitty small group. We could have gone over there with our pieces and blown the whole big apartment building where the little old popguns was comin' from. But ain't nobody got no pistols, no shotguns, no nothin', and you got to get the hell out of the way."

This is a Lord that felt naked going over there without a piece. Nevertheless, he said:

"The Lords aren't just goin' lookin' for trouble. We could wipe that group out but there would be a lot of separate incidents. Nine years ago we would have got our pieces together and went over there with the war wagon. We'd go over there and wipe it out, like molotov cocktails, everything. Stand there and shoot all the windows from top to bottom with shotguns and what not. The babies get shot; the women they get shot; the grandfathers and grandmothers they get shot rockin' in the chair by the window. We would have made a parking lot of the building.

But that's an irresponsible way of thinking even though that's what they do in Vietnam, because you hurt a lot of innocent people for no reason. Like the guy who burned down the tavern. There was one guy in there that he felt mistreated him and he burned up everybody in the whole tavern. All he know was that it was the joint he got kicked out of a little while ago, felt mistreated, went and got some gas and come back and burned the joint down with everybody in it. Now everybody in there didn't mistreat him.

"We didn't want that irresponsible thinking with the Black Aces. We are strong as any. We don't have to take low to none, but we don't want to just go and wipe off places. On the other hand, we can't let some group come up and just threaten everything we got started."

Like others, Calvin feels the uncertainty of living in the neighborhood. "Look at me, I always got to carry this big old knife, man. What the fuck I need to carry this for, and I'm married too? I don't want to be bothered with this shit, but still inside of me I believe if the Vice Lords have to roll down on anything, I have to roll with 'em because they been a part of me all my life."

His partner, Jerry, also knows that this fighting is not the way things should be but "this has been our thing all our life. I got married too and moved right here on Millard, through the alley. Now if something really goes down, like the Black Aces comin' around here, I'm gonna be on the back porch with my German Luger. They say they came through there the other night and shot at Al, and I say, OK, wait; I'm gonna stand out there and burn one. I'm not gonna burn to kill; I'm gonna hit him in the leg and show him that we all over here. I swear I don't want no gangbanging. I don't want it at all. But if somethin' happens around the neighborhood that we feel we should go down with, they know we will be there.''

In a meeting with the Black Aces in 1969, Bobby explained what we were trying to do:

''The things that we're doing to each other, we can't have that no more. Had we not been worried about little cats like these little dudes settin' up in these front rows, and then we got the little sisters out on the street, man—had this been somethin' like six years ago, man, we'd be in worse shape than the South Side because it's time.

''We've had more trouble trying to stop cats from comin' around messin' in the streets and we know where quite a few of you cats live. But what we're trying to create here, man, is that Vice Lords, Black Aces, Black Panthers, whatever you have, the name shouldn't make any difference. What should make the difference is black people. Otherwise that honky is going to conquer. We shouldn't get out here and me and you get in an argument and run and get our guns and shoot at each other about a name calling or because I jumped on your little brother. For everything that happens, there has to be a reason, and if we really look at things the problem is not among ourselves. The things we argue and fuss and fight over is not comin' from us; it's comin' from the environment—the way we live, the food we eat, the clothes we got to wear, the amount of money in our pockets. If none of this is suitable, then we gonna leave home with an attitude, and if a brother just say maybe an iota of something out of the way, damn, you ready to jump on him or to get in trouble some kinda way.

''But now the brother is not the problem. The problem is somewhere else. So what we're tryin to create here is an understanding so we can deal with the problem.

''Now I'm not gonna say that bygones are gonna be bygones. As long as you got people, you gonna have cats that just don't dig dudes. Well, honkies the same way. You got honkies that don't like other honkies, you understand, but they learn to get away from this kind of thing if it's a thing that's gonna help them. Whereas me and you get out here and kill each other for a few words. We gotta get to the point where we don't get mad about so much.

''Our problems come from way back. Our problems started with my father's father and maybe his father's father. We got to find out why we get so mad. Why do I run and get me a pistol and shoot this cat, and he live next door to me for seven years and I know him and I ain't really had nothin' against him except for this little incident? When the police get you and put you in jail, the incident wasn't really that big, but it was that spur of the moment anger. And it didn't come from the brother— it was within you all along, jack, and as long as we stand around these corners and take potshots at each other, we ain't gonna never make it.

"The gangs get the people that the parents don't have time for. The gang gets the high school dropout. The gangs get the people who are comin' out of jails. The gangs get all the stickup men, the dope addicts. As far as the system is concerned, the gangs are constructed of nothing but what the system cannot use, and they class this as garbage.

"Any time a youngster gets with anything that has a gang label they are just lost people. There is no hope. What we're trying to prove is that there is some good, and a lot of talent is going to waste right here with what the system says is no good. Our first priority is to show that we do have enough sense to do something.

"There is a way of dealing with problems. We can all go down with our pieces in our hands, or we could try and deal with this cat one way or another to make sure that there will be some black survival after the thing is over.

"There are sacrifices that will have to be made. I might very well lose my life because I'm sick of it too. What we're trying to create is an organization that will deal with our problems. We want to stop seeing our little brothers and sisters starving to death and getting inferior education and living in these rat- and roach-infested houses."

The Black P Stones have experienced the same thing we have and we get along. They have had many a guy bite the dust. They are blacks, we are black. And that gives us brotherhood. They may be Stones and we are Lords, but we can all get together and ball that fist up and throw that black power sign.

Bobby has said that "we feel like whatever or whoever is speaking of tryin to pull the black people up to the right standards of living, we shouldn't hesitate to form a coalition or to give some kind of support." We have had many people come and ask for support but before we make a move, we always investigate. We never just jump out the window. If it's a no good program, then we don't participate. But if it's something for the good of blacks, then we'll give support because this is what we should have been doing a long time ago.

Bobby says, "What we are doing right now is something that should have been done a long time ago—trying to save the youth, trying to preserve black people, trying to pull us up to our rightful standards of living.

"There is violence out here but there's also violence in white folks neighborhoods. A cat might be thinking that it was alright for him to rip somebody off. It's been done before and the cat don't amount to nothin'—he's a black cat, a gang member—so I rip him off and it don't mean nothin' . . . it's just another cat that white folks don't have to kill or deal with.

"But now, with a white boy, that's different. I've been taught to respect that white man because he can cause me all the trouble that I ever thought I can get. I was taught to fear the white, but I don't know nothin' about showing respect to a black brother so I would eliminate him, cut his throat or shoot him . . . it's just like crushing a roach."

This is what we're trying to keep down. But when there is going to be a fight, everybody comes with guns instead of bricks and bottles and sticks like before. We're pretty well organized and if something happens in another neighborhood, we'll try to iron out the problem. If we find out who did something we will call the police.

Cupid says, "We done cut loose that prehistoric way of takin' care of our own business 'cause we found out if somebody killed one of us and we gonna kill him, all they do is take another one of us away. So we got different polices we work with and when we find out, we just take 'em over there."

Cupid feels that all wars are not won fighting. "There has been a time when we had to kill or shoot, but nowdays we win wars with our mind. You can win a war without killing, and that's why I feel we're the kings. And being king gets you lovers, people that love you for what you're doin' and want to help you do it. We love each other and we don't want to see nobody hurt each other."

We don't know how long we're going to exist before the monster swallows us up. We're not out to fight Daley or Nixon. We're out to help people. But if it comes to where there is no other alternative (and that point is coming when we'll have to change our structure and deal with that), we'll have to stop writing proposals. We'll have to stop sitting down at tables with people talking with forked tongues.

We can stop Daley's voting power on the West Side all the way from the Loop to Cicero. The Daley machine is very strong, but we can crack it because we are the people that he was using. There's nobody else after us.

We're not just trying to save poor black people. We're trying to set up a system that helps poor Mexican, poor white, poor Indian, poor people in general. We are going to get together because we are going to die together.

The Lords would have gone for just what we are going for now years ago if we were able. But we weren't able. We didn't have what it takes. But now, slowly but surely, we progressed. But you can't do nothin' with nothin', so Goat looks around at what's happening and wonders what will become of us:

"White people are probably not ready to hear what has to be done. You could tell 'em a lotta things. I don't think it would do any good. I don't think right now that those type of people are ready for what's coming. They haven't had enough taste of violence.

"They got so much chaos they can't see what's going on. They gonna wake up one morning and there gonna stand the dragon. You know, spittin' that fire, and they gonna be throwin' the buckets of water, but it's gonna be too late."

Nothin' Left But Death*

In 1979, there was a vacant lot where we used to have a restaurant and a two story street mural; iron grates secured a building that once was a walk-in art studio and classroom. Cupid, Pep, Goat, J.W., and many, many more were dead. Those that weren't dead returned to the roulette of life in which homicide is the leading cause of death for black male teenagers.

In the summer of 1967, I went to Chicago to evaluate federally-funded summer programs. When I learned that Vice Lords ran the West Side streets, I let several people know I wanted to meet these Lords and then tried to be easy to find. My first contact came at a rally to raise money for the poor people of Mississippi — an event that in the summer of 1967 found police standing by in riot gear and buses. The rally was all black, but I went in, and somewhere into the speeches, a hand touched my shoulder and a voice told me to go into the lobby if I wanted to meet the Lords.

After a brief talk, a Vice Lord chief asked me to meet them on Sunday afternoon at the Lawndale Pool Room; they would guarantee my getting out unharmed. That may sound reassuring, but until then I hadn't been thinking about getting hurt. The pool room meeting resulted in a summer of sharing. I moved into the Kedzie YMCA but hung out on Sixteenth Street. I was supposed to tell Vice Lords at the pool room when I was ready to leave, but often I walked to the YMCA after midnight rather than bother somebody for a ride.

One night when several voices called out from the shadows, I recognized a Vice Lord who had made no secret of his contempt for whites. I thought my time had come, but instead, they told me I was out of my mind for walking the streets' alone, then escorted me to the Central Park bus so the Chief wouldn't have their heads for not taking care of the honky.

* Written by David Dawley in 1979 as a ten year retrospective.

The Vice Lords got a reputation as violent for good reason, but discounting the Lords as simply vicious prevents us from understanding who, what, and why they are. They are dropouts, delinquents, hard core; they are thieves, burglars, muggers, murderers. They are branded: incorrigible, sociopath, psychopath. Labels that are easy to get, hard to remove. They are the people society gave up on — the bottom of the barrel.

Yet these Lords, and the many street people like them, are also people who want love, respect, responsibility and friendship. They are like most young people, growing up with many of the same personal needs. For most, the gang is the only real family they know; the gang is survival, protection, recognition, education.

Just as the Boy Scouts did for me, the Vice Lords provide identification and support for teenagers on the street. The tragic difference between my childhood in New England and the life of Vice Lords in Chicago is the ghetto — the inner city quicksand of social and economic oppression.

But in 1967, Vice Lord leaders like Bobby Gore decided they'd had enough; too many were dead, maimed, and in prison — too many were still left on the same corner. During that summer, I saw these street people struggle to change, and I watched government and local business finesse these efforts with all the smoothness my background prepared me to recognize.

When my work was finished, I returned to Washington knowing that I couldn't walk away from what I'd seen. Though these were years when whites were getting thrown out of windows by militant blacks, and despite agreeing in principle with the prevailing thought that whites should organize whites, not blacks, I had discovered that the Vice Lords needed help only I seemed prepared to give. While they felt deep bitterness toward white society, the Vice Lords were not ideologues; they made friends or enemies with individual people. Instead of the hostility I expected, I found friendship. Consequently, I returned to Chicago as a free lance organizer with a plan for converting street power into organized community action.

The city was dark when I arrived, but I remember a welcome sign that proclaimed ''Richard J. Daley, Mayor'' — my last welcome from the Mayor who later declared official war on gangs. In those days, I was supposed to be some kind of radical for working with a street gang, or a ''tear jerkin' liberal'' as the Captain of Gang Intelligence thought. In fact, I was mostly a basic Eagle Scout/Peace Corps activist who didn't like hypocrisy, racism or oppression. I didn't start with SDS[1] ideology but with the hard reality of Chicago streets.

In the next two years, we demonstrated how a group with effective leadership could transform destructive energy into constructive progress. We put briefcases in hands that used to hold wine; we grew grass where the sun didn't shine; we gave hope to people who didn't dare to dream.

We opened "The African Lion," a boutique to sell Afro-American clothing, a business to encourage pride in black history and to expose black residents of the West Side to the rich heritage of Africa, not as a separatist movement but as a search for meaning. We opened "Teen Town," an ice cream parlor restaurant at a location described by one newspaper as having "more problems for a square block than any other in the city." Teen Town was a symbol for what youth could achieve.

A Management Training Institute tried to prepare Vice Lords to administer business and neighborhood programs. Art & Soul — a joint venture with the Museum of Contemporary Art — responded to the Kerner Commission warning that "our nation is moving toward two societies, one black, one white" by building friendship between black and white artists. "The House of Lords" was a hang-in to offer an alternative to the corner. With ping pong, card tables, jukebox, and books, the House of Lords was a place to sleep, study, dance, or just stay warm in the winter.

There were more programs, even a national coalition with similar street organizations, and as in all of the other activities, blacks controlled and whites helped as new partnerships were built into programs before this concept became more widely accepted. Furthermore, while trying to create opportunity for individuals to develop potential, CVL Inc. at the same time was trying to change "the system" — a strategy of economic, educational, and political development.

Organizing programs is more demanding and tedious than merely complaining about what the city hasn't done, but the work was not without humor. I remember one meeting when executives from the Leo Burnett advertising agency came out to help design a report to the public. As the sun set slowly on the ghetto, I watched usually confident executives begin to squirm. I knew they were too fearful to admit that they wanted to get out of there before dark, but since one was a friend from college I didn't end the meeting until our business was finished.

I saw several Vice Lords sitting on my car so I decided to confirm the advertisers' worst fears.

[1] Students for a Democratic Society, a national organization of mostly white radical students, founded in Port Huron, Michigan in 1962.

Since game playing is an important element of street life, I told them to get off my car. In a mock showdown, the accommodating Lords threatened to "dust" our white asses while my advertising friends pleaded with me to let them in the car. Later, I confessed, but these tycoons of Michigan Avenue went to work the next day with a new view of mortality.

Unfortunately, there was tragedy too. As one friend said, you don't have to look for trouble, trouble finds you. Sixteenth and Lawndale was one of those places. We could write a book about that corner — crap games behind "the iron curtain," Richard's Wild Irish in a brown bag with tributes poured to dead Lords, Fourth of July barbecues and dancing in the street — a corner where Walter Cronkite's network news filmed our grass for the nation to admire.

As for me, a few interesting moments but no scars. A gunshot lodged in my car window; one Vice Lord pointed a pistol to my head and threatened to blow my head off if I didn't apologize for something or other; friends were hit with shotgun pellets while sitting on the steps of the house next to mine and some girls set fire to my first apartment.

But I liked the people I lived with, and I miss the excitement of street life — the stoop sitting, pool shooting, shouting and carryin' on, the neighborhood love that came together in a Christmas dinner where the turkey was kept warm on a pool room radiator. I lived on the first floor of what newspapers called Bloody Sixteenth Street, and I felt safe because I knew friends were watching.

When I left in 1969, the Vice Lords had money; there were no street crises, no pending trials. The Lords knew how to develop an idea into a program, how to write a proposal, where to go for money in Chicago, Washington, or New York and how to run a program.

I left in good times, not bad, and I left because I'd done what I wanted to do: to start a process by which a few people could begin to shape a new future. As with the Peace Corps, after living with the Vice Lords, I felt kin to Lawrence when he said he felt "estranged from the English yet not wholly one with the Arabs."

Like the YMCA and other social agencies, the Vice Lords depended heavily on private philanthropy, but in late 1969, technical changes in the laws of philanthropy cut the flow of support by restricting foundation grants to organizations that were not tax exempt. Though non profit, the Vice Lords had been waiting two years for Internal Revenue Service approval of a pending tax exempt application. Not surprisingly, Watergate investigations revealed that "Conservative Vice Lords, Inc."

appeared on a special target list at the Internal Revenue Service, providing confirmation that tax exemption had been stonewalled as a tactic in the Nixon administration's repression of activist black organizations.

During this time, Vietnam became expensive, Nixon withheld appropriated funds for social programs,[2] and companies got back to business as usual as corporate profits went from black to red.

Whether you're the YMCA or the Vice Lords, no matter how dedicated you are, programs close when there's no money for rent, lights and phones. For the Vice Lords in 1970, there was no public money, no private money, no place to turn.

In Chicago, though Mayor Daley had been president of a street gang, his attitude was reflected in the comment of his Chief of Gang Intelligence: "they are hard core criminals; they are not redeemable, and anybody who thinks they are is wasting his time." He might have said they all look alike.

As these truths became painfully clear, many "concerned citizens" moved on to cleaning up the environment, the new romance for the early seventies, and some businessmen pulled out when they heard Attorney General John Mitchell's threats of repression. With the Chicago Seven conspiracy trial of 1970, the rumors of IRS audits were too believable for comfort.

Official Chicago, and eventually the media, tainted Vice Lord achievements with Blackstone Ranger scandals. Though the Vice Lords felt brotherhood with the Stones, there were significant differences in what was happening and what was accomplished during this period. The tendency of even good reporters to run the stories together reminded me of similar mistakes in reporting about Southeast Asia: where North Vietnamese, Viet Cong, Cambodians, and Laotians were considered a monolithic communist threat rather than a collection of separate nationalities, interests, and politics.

In 1979, the street seemed a bombed out wreck, an urban cemetery to a short-lived hope. Close friends were dead, locked up or hanging on with a needle, a hustle, a prayer. Of the leaders, only Bobby Gore

---

[2] In *The Power Game*, Hedrick Smith writes that following Richard Nixon's election in 1968, "House Democrats under Speaker John McCormack fought Nixon tooth and nail on domestic spending. Nixon's defiant stand that he did not have to spend all the funds that Congress voted for social programs left McCormack and company little choice but to fight to protect the institutional powers of Congress. The showdowns over federal spending grew so heated that Congress finally passed the Budget and Impoundment Act of 1974 to force future presidents to abide by congressional appropriations.

survived, but his price for freedom had been ten years as a political prisoner in the Illinois State Penitentiary at Joliet. The tuition for his high school and two college degrees was becoming number C-01479 in a James Cagney prison that is not on my approved list of places to spend the night. Even so, Bobby demonstrated an unrelenting gut determination to survive, to grow — an inspiration to the many young people he urged to give up territorial jealousies, to stop violence, to find a better way.

Many will consider those few beautiful years in the sixties a failure for the Vice Lords; in fact, a failure of the Vice Lords. Like others, I know the shattered dream, but with so many changes in the country, I realize there was no way for anyone, particularly struggling street people, to hold together what was built in 1969.

The Vice Lords had converted grants into jobs and community service, but storefronts and programs were only the visible surface of deeper changes.

In two years, the outlaws of the ghetto had moved into business development and direct political action — the kind of tough and legitimate fighting for social change that propelled Chicago's Irish into power. So when the Vice Lords helped to form the vanguard of a coalition that closed $100 million of construction to negotiate more blacks into the trade unions, Mayor Daley understood the deeper political message.

For street gangsters who couldn't have cared less a few years before, this standing up to the system was a healthy challenge. They were growing out of neighborhood fights about turf into aggressive action for social change. There was more black consciousness, less gang consciousness; there was more unity among blacks and more bridges to whites.

The Vice Lords got respect, recognition and cooperation. They were considered tough, ambitious and positive, and that image was backstopped with no riot since the death of Martin Luther King, Jr. and less crime as Sixteenth Street was safe to walk. Young Vice Lords had higher expectations for justice and for how whites relate to blacks. They began to feel good about themselves and that feeling was immeasurably important to building a new future.

These achievements — in image, behavior, attitudes and service to the community — occurred in the face of institutional hostility and sometimes outright injustice. Growing as they were, the Vice Lords might have continued to develop new opportunity for young people on the West Side. They were on the way, but there was not enough help and too little time. In my judgment, as a country we failed the Vice Lords, and worse, we failed ourselves.

We are left to wonder if there is anything different today to tell the Lords of whatever name that life can change. The Three Mile Island bomb didn't go off in Lawndale, but every day people die from the fallout of our neglect.

The programs developed in the sixties are not necessarily appropriate to replicate, but somewhere beyond the energy crisis, inflation crisis and budget crisis, the country needs a wake up call, a kick in the conscience to mobilize a new generation of caring people.

Spittin' That Fire

In the last chapter of *A Nation Of Lords*, Goat said that white people are not ready to hear what has to be done: "They gonna wake up one morning and there gonna stand the dragon. You know, spittin' that fire, and they gonna be throwin' the buckets of water, but it's gonna be too late."

Now in 1992, as we sprint to the beginning of a new century, the dragon is smokin' crack cocaine, gangs are shooting automatic weapons, the police are outnumbered and parents fear for the health and safety of their children.

As the eighties closed, drugs had become big business, and some gangs had started to fight for market share as well as turf. In another era, territory defined power, but today cash is the currency of colors. To the three m's of the street: mind, mouth and muscle is added a fourth — money. Not so different from the greed and glory of Wall Street.

In Lawndale, a generation has been slaughtered by neglect — dead from bullets, dope and all the reasons that keep the ghetto an urban swamp for sensible, sane and secure people to avoid. In October, 1985, reporters Mark Zambrano and William Recktenwald wrote in the Chicago Tribune:

> In many respects, North Lawndale typifies what has happened to the black slums of urban America over the last two decades as jobs have left, the economy has soured, housing has crumbled and the ranks of those dependent on government handouts have soared. The lives of many here are mired in a daily routine of alcohol, crime, drugs and the underground economy.
>
> In North Lawndale, the population dropped by more than 30,000 from 1975-1985 and the percentage of people living there on welfare rose by more than 45 percent.
>
> Over the last 10 years, 80 percent, of the manufacturing jobs have left the community. Wholesale and retail jobs have dropped by 44 percent. Work

in the service sector, the fastest growing sector in the nation's economy, has declined by 1,087 positions.

The murder rate here is 5 times the national average, sexual assault is 6 times the average and other serious assaults are 10 times the average.

Here in North Lawndale, where many of the residents belong to the black underclass, it is not difficult to find people whose lives have been swallowed up by the urban wasteland around them and who have been down and out for so very long that their basic instinct is to adapt, not escape.

A street word for death is "wasted," but to me, wasted is people with enormous talent, locked in the bowels of a city, trapped in a life of underclass pain.

In the sixties, ghettos exploded with riots as "Burn, Baby, Burn!" became a recurring nightmare for white America. In the seventies, the inner city imploded like a controlled demolition. Drugs, despair and hustles were the ashes of broken dreams. In the eighties, although crack cocaine didn't pervade Chicago like other cities, the streets again exploded in a feeding frenzy of fast money and drugs.

A few years earlier, if you got out of line, you might get a Sixteenth Street whipping, but you'd live to tell. Today, you get killed. From the wilding attack in Central Park on a woman jogger to drive-by shootings, street culture has developed violent variations of teenage conformity — demonstrating in prime time the collective savagery that William Golding depicted in *Lord Of The Flies*.

Former drug czar, William Bennett, talked about "bad people." But most are not bad people. They're people growing up in bad conditions who have learned to do bad things. He says there's no work ethic on the street, but gang members are not only "wannabes;" they're "wannahaves." Many work hard; they just work at the wrong thing. Though most are dropouts and in danger of becoming unemployable in the new workforce, they still want what the American dream promises. If given a chance, most will respond and if there's hope, many will try.

Criminal behavior cannot be condoned, but gangs, drugs and violence will continue until we deal with underlying conditions of housing, health, education and employment. Gang members are simply visible symbols of the failure of families, schools and public policy to provide educational and economic opportunity.

I'd like to give my friends in Lawndale a reason not to push dope, stick needles or sell bodies, but national priorities are often dictated by events rather than determined by need. We punished Iraq for ravaging Kuwait, but we have ignored the scorched earth in our own cities. We worry about having Japan as a landlord yet the physical and social infrastructure of our country is crumbling. Water supplies, sewers, roads and bridges are leaking, cracking and falling down while hopelessness and helplessness are attitudes shared by gang members and common citizens who feel that the problems of inner cities are too overwhelming to fix.

We're a nation of self-centered consumers who face a crisis of the American dream, the belief that we'll always get more, that our destiny is secure, that for us, there are no limits. Now, if we are to emerge from the selfishness of the eighties, we need to accept personal responsibility for rebuilding a sense of community. This is not simply a matter of conscience. Today, the cost of locking out inner city youth is a lower quality of life for all Americans. What we confront are issues of national security and economic competitiveness as well as personal and community safety — issues that determine whether we can compete in a global economy and whether future generations will enjoy the prosperity that many of us took for granted as children.

Giving Vice Lords and other gang members the opportunity for positive participation in community life is essential in the face of a shrinking workforce. And the preparation of that workforce is driving every plan for survival in global economy. As Louis Gerstner, Chairman of RJR Nabisco has said, "there's no such thing as a successful company in an unsuccessful society."

In Lawndale, a generation ago, we tried to develop the opportunity for an individual to realize his potential, to help him recognize a responsibility to his community, to create situations that would reward new behaviors and higher expectations.

The model of a street corporation preserved the identity of a group while shifting the governing norms and values. The strategy was to motivate young people with jobs, service and eventually political action. The hope was to change lives, and the goal was to change society so that opportunity and justice would prevail over oppression and exploitation.

Ironically, the slogan "Power *to* the People" in the sixties gave birth to power *of* the people in the eighties — in the Philippines, Poland, Hungary, Czechoslovakia, Rumania and East Germany — far from Lawndale where there will be more years of frustration before our own citizens are liberated from poverty and racism.

Two decades have passed since we grew grass on Sixteenth and Lawndale, and as one Vice Lord says, "there ain't nothin' but the past." Nevertheless, we must persevere because if we stop trying, there is no hope, and without hope, our decline may look like Humpty Dumpty's fall. There are many interconnected challenges — gangs, drugs, families, schools, jobs — but education is pivotal to almost every long run hope for change. Unless schools find ways to reduce the number of thrownouts and drop outs, the streets will become a landfill of locked-out youth who are attracted to gangs, and the dragon will spit his fire into your home and mine.

In foreign affairs, Desert Storm demonstrated the power of defined goals, massive force and political resolve. Now the question is: can we mobilize similar political commitment and economic investment in a coordinated campaign to bring opportunity, hope and justice to the Third World within our own borders.

The Only White Vice Lord
by Bobby Gore

I met Dave in the summer of 1967 when we were putting on a fundraiser for poor counties in Mississippi at the Senate Theater. We were busy trying to keep security when I looked up and here this guy had come over on Kedzie and Madison at night during the Black Power era. And he came by himself—nobody brought him. With all the bad press we were getting, I thought he was a gutsy guy for being there.

A few days later, Pep brought him through the pool room. He was working for TransCentury in Washington D.C., doing a study for the government, and he needed four or five guys to work with him. We were to do a door-to-door canvas with printed questionnaires so we went through training and how we should present ourselves.

This questionnaire asked how youth felt about different agencies. Were they doing a good job? Did they have meaningful programs? Then there were questions about playgrounds—Did they have equipment? baseballs? basketballs? That's when we found out there had been millions of dollars poured into Lawndale to reach young people on the street, which at that time was the so-called gangs.

We decided to check out a few centers, wanting to know how much had come to the street—not necessarily money but what programs— maybe basketball teams, baseball teams—only to find out these people were afraid of us. Even though we didn't go to college, when things are not right, you can tell. And this is what activated Dave too—he had some idea of what was supposed to be going on.

A lot happened during that summer. Dave was hanging around and saw that we were serious in wanting to rid the community of crime and violence so when he had to go back to TransCentury and make out his reports, he promised to return to Sixteenth Street to help us.

199

A couple months passed and the next thing we know, Dave popped up again. Just the sight of this guy coming back told us he was sincere.

Dave started going out with us, and you can imagine what the reaction was when we went into an all black dance hall—not disco, but dance hall—and Dave's the only white guy in there. The place was full of blacks, but Dave had as much fun as we did.

I began to put a lot of trust in this guy. He was razor sharp and dedicated to making our ideas become a reality. But there was always a danger for Dave being a white guy, running around Sixteenth Street, the West Side. He was living on the street, just like we were, and there were a lot of Lords that wanted to hurt him. In fact, there was a policeman we used to call Gloves who wanted Dave off the streets.* This guy was known for breaking heads, just beating people: "get off the goddamn corner; I'm not gonna ask ya but one time," and if you didn't move, this guy had either knocked you down or kicked you in the rear.

We weren't goin' for a lot of that—as a matter of fact, part of our move was to contact police commanders in Marquette and Fillmore to let them know we were going to improve the community—cut out the gangbanging. But people like Gloves and some of the Lords who were snatching pocketbooks had a hard time accepting Dave. Some wondered what is this guy doing? Is he an FBI plant? Is he out to crush us? So we put out a communication that if anything happened to Dave, it had to happen to all of us.

Dave started coming up with some possible answers to what we were trying to organize, and after hearing what Dave was saying to some of the people he said he would contact, I started believing that he was really going to give us some help.

As time went on, Dave became more involved with both the street life and our programs—to the point that he used to get downright angry when we wouldn't get off our butts and do what we were supposed to be carrying out. And that was another learning thing from Dave. When you got something to do, you were supposed to go ahead and do it.

I can remember the time when Dr. King was assassinated. That was another night of total chaos. Looting, burning, the whole bit. And Dave was out in the middle with us—passing out handbills, saying this ain't the way to do it: we're destroyin our own property—we're hurting the neighborhood, and that's not what Dr. King would have wanted.

---

* Gloves Davis was reported to have killed Mark Clark in the Black Panther killings in 1969. The Cook County District Attorney's Office was condemned, and years later, the government paid nearly $2 million in an out of court settlement with the families of those who were killed.

Dave was out there in the streets with us, and that was a very dangerous situation for him. But the cat was a trooper — he was a real live Lord then. Everybody knew him by that time, and they knew that this cat was always up front. Some carried little suspicions, but they were beginning to relax with Dave. And that wasn't because of what we said earlier. That was because Dave was part of what was going on.

Another time, we had occasion to go to East St. Louis. We were working on a national program called Y.O.U. Basically, it was black. There were some whites there that were sincere like Dave, but one of the guys from East St. Louis stood up and said: "We don't want any whites in this meeting — they gotta get out."

Well, the Lords, being from Chicago, had to take a stand. We just made the statement: "OK, if this guy that's with us has to go, we won't even be a part of this ourselves." So by us being a leader in this whole concept of Youth Organizations United — opening communication, one group learning from another — when they asked that all whites leave the room, we just made a decision that if Dave had to go, we'd go too. So a vote was taken, and we won. Dave and all other whites were allowed to stay and as a result, YOU was born and became a reality.

We stood up for Dave because at that point, he had become a part of us. We weren't lookin' at color; this guy had become a regular.

I heard time and time again what is this honky doin' over here — "he ain't gonna do nothin' but go off and write his book." We heard it from policemen, from Vice Lords, from some white liberals — jealous people. What they didn't know is that Dave put time in and he had the right to do the book. Hell, Dave couldn't write the book if he hadn't lived this shit. And the good part is that the book was done under contract, and some of the profits would be channeled back into scholarships.

I was locked up when Dave went back to Boston. I was in the wrong place at the wrong damn time and some killing went on. I ended up being convicted for a crime I didn't commit. Our biggest fear had been something just like what happened — that the people would come in and crush the whole thing.

I served 11 years and 3 months in Stateville, and I was in communication with Dave on a fairly regular basis while I was incarcerated. Even through the letters that this guy would write, you could feel warmth and concern. The guy made some moves for me and even came down during my parole hearing.

Today, though we're living in different cities, we share the memories of having worked to turn the Vice Lords into a constructive organization, of helping to make the streets safe, of providing hope to the hard core that society gave up on.

After twenty years, we're still brothers.

While in the Stateville Penitentiary in Joliet, Illinois, Bobby Gore completed high school and college and founded a chapter of the Jaycees inside Stateville. Since his parole, he has worked for the Safer Foundation in Chicago, a nonprofit job placement and counseling service for ex-convicts. He has been honored as Safer's Employee of the Year and while Director of the Cabrini-Green Outreach Center as Manager of the Year.

In Memory

Since the summer of 1967, many have died — dead by murder, dead from drugs, dead by Sixteenth Street where trouble doesn't rest. In these names is the truth that a generation has been lost and that homicide is the leading cause of death among black male teenagers.

Alfonso	Hosea
Pep	King Freddie
Goat	Black Jesus
Cupid	Elzy
J.W.	Lonnie
Calloway	"Happy Stick" Tabb
Billy Washington	Lee Cross
Doc Brown	Elgie
Boomer	Joyce
Monk	Dini
Wayne	Jesse Heath
Big Carl	Ronald Love
Satan	Little Ricky
Duke Jackson	Sporty
Little Fool	Duke Capone
Duane Patterson	Shotgun
Little Lord	Tex
Linky	Caveman
Joe Gangster	Li'l Jesse
Demetrius	Phyllis
Little Herc	Tiger
Son	

In the beginning the incoming organizer must establish his identity or, putting it another way, get his license to operate. He must have a reason for being there—a reason acceptable to the people

His acceptance as an organizer depends on his success in convincing key people—and many others—first, that he is on their side, and second, that he has ideas and knows how to fight to change things; that he's not one of these guys "doing his thing," that he's a winner. Otherwise who needs him? All his presence means is that the census changes from 225,000 to 225,001.

It is not enough to persuade them of your competence, talents and courage—they must have faith in your ability and courage. They must believe in your capacity not just to provide the opportunity for action, power, change, adventure, a piece of the drama of life, but to give a very definite promise, almost an assurance of victory. They must also have faith in your courage to fight the oppressive establishment.

Saul Alinsky
Rules For Radicals

Alfonso   Dave   Pep

David Dawley is a businessman, consultant and nationally recognized community organizer. He lived in Lawndale for two years from 1967 through 1969 where he was known as the only white Vice Lord. In 1968, Esquire Magazine selected him as one of "Twenty Seven People Worth Saving," and the Governor of Massachusetts later nominated him as one of "Greater Boston's Ten Outstanding Young Leaders."

A native of Westminster, Massachusetts, he is a graduate of Dartmouth College, the University of Michigan and the Harvard Business School. As a Peace Corps Volunteer in 1963, he worked in community development in Honduras. In 1970, President Nixon appointed him to the National Advisory Council of the Peace Corps, and in 1980 President Carter appointed him to the White House Conference on Small Business.

He is Chairman of The National Center for Gang Policy, an advisor to the Family and Youth Services Bureau of the Department of Health and Human Services and a consultant to NIKE, RJR Nabisco's NEXT CENTURY SCHOOLS and Cassidy & Associates.

He identifies with Saul Alinsky's comment that an organizer is driven by the desire to create and with John LeCarre who said "A desk is a dangerous place from which to watch the world."

© 1991 Stuart Bratesman.